Sixth edition

Palabra por palabra

Spanish vocabulary for Edexcel A-level

Mike Thacker
Phil Turk

Acknowledgements

Mike Thacker would like to thank Sebastián Bianchi for his support and for his helpful elucidation of some Spanish items.

Orders: please contact Bookpoint Ltd, 130 Park Drive, Milton Park, Abingdon, Oxon OX14 4SE. Telephone: (44) 01235 827827. Fax: (44) 01235 400401. E-mail education@bookpoint.co.uk Lines are open from 9 a.m. to 5 p.m., Monday to Saturday, with a 24-hour message answering service. You can also order through our website: www.hoddereducation.co.uk

ISBN: 978 1 5104 3483 7

First published in 1992 by
Hodder Education,
An Hachette UK Company
Carmelite House
50 Victoria Embankment
London EC4Y 0DZ
www.hoddereducation.co.uk

Second edition published 1996
Third edition published 2000
Fourth edition published 2006
Fifth edition published 2010
This sixth edition published 2018

Impression number 10 9 8 7 6 5 4 3 2 1
Year 2023 2022 2021 2020 2019 2018

Cover photo © roberharding/Alamy
Typeset in India
Printed by CPI Group (UK) Ltd, Croydon, CR0 4YY

A catalogue record for this title is available from the British Library.

Contents

Introduction

This sixth edition of *Palabra por palabra* has been substantially revised to reflect changes in the Edexcel AS and A-level examination specifications and contemporary topics. It contains a wealth of up-to-date, useful vocabulary, taken from printed and online publications for each of the topic areas, as well as new and updated sections:

- **Section A**, *Quiero decir…*, provides a vocabulary framework for developing a theme either orally or in writing.
- **Section B** deals with 'false friends', words that may not mean what their immediate appearance might suggest.
- **Section C** offers help in choosing the correct equivalent for English words with several meanings and gives alternatives to some overused words.
- **Section D** contains a range of vocabulary to support essay writing on film and literature.
- **Section E** contains three extra lists on the topics of Sport, the Environment and Fashion, which are not included in the Edexcel specification; should you choose one of these topics for the Individual Research Project (examined orally), the vocabulary will give you useful support.
- **Section F** gives a list of useful, mainly abstract, verbs, which you could well need, but which don't fit easily under any topic heading.

The core of the book consists of vocabulary lists relating to four major Edexcel themes, each of which is divided into three sections, each covering a topic from the Edexcel specification. These are divided further into specific social and cultural topics. At the end of each theme you will find:

- some useful websites, which deal with or provide links to aspects of the particular topics
- two or three exercises based on the relevant theme that practise the vocabulary listed therein, together with some strategies to help you to learn it

The method of this book is to list words and phrases in an order that follows the logic of a lesson about, or a discussion of, various aspects of each topic. The topics covered match those in the Edexcel A-level specification and, as such, this book is ideal to use alongside any textbook for the course, particularly in order to prepare for your oral examination. All theme-based vocabulary has been included with the aim of using it in an oral register.

All sections have been divided into manageable subsections, and cross-references are provided where relevant vocabulary may occur in more than one chapter.

The following abbreviations have been used:

- *LAm* (Latin America)
- *Sp* (Spain)
- *adj* (adjective)
- *adv* (adverb)
- *coll* (colloquial)
- *f* (feminine)
- *indic* (indicative)
- *inf* (infinitive)
- *trans* (transitive)
- *intrans* (intransitive)
- *lit* (literally)
- *n* (noun)
- *pl* (plural)
- *pres* (present)
- *subj* (subjunctive)
- *v* (verb)

Learning vocabulary

As an advanced language student, you will by now be aware that words are the tools of the trade. However sound your knowledge of grammar and facts, and however brilliant your ideas, you cannot express them without the necessary words! And unlike when you learnt your mother tongue, unless you are extremely lucky, you won't be surrounded by people speaking Spanish 24/7. More likely your contact will be limited to a few hours of Spanish classes per week. Try, however, to increase your contact through websites, satellite broadcasts, newspapers, magazines or other materials in Spanish that you can lay your hands on. This little book provides you with a good selection of words and phrases on the topics you will encounter, but you should also keep your own vocabulary notebook (paper or electronic) and record, as far as possible under topic headings, any further ones you come across.

Vocabulary learning is a highly personal process and each of us will discover the method that suits us best. However, you must accept that it won't 'stick' without some positive effort on your part. The important thing is to experiment and find the method that works best for you. And, by the way, 'method' is the key word: you must be methodical.

The following hints might help:

- Don't try to absorb too much at once: 20 words might be sufficient, possibly fewer.
- You will need to check these several times, at intervals, marking the ones you know.
- Take a break or do something else, then check again.
- Check them yet again before learning the next batch.
- Work alone, checking yourself, or get a friend or family member to test you.
- Don't let lists of words accumulate. Better to learn little and often.
- Use the words you have learnt in your written and spoken work: 'use them or lose them' applies here.

You can also expand your vocabulary by taking a word and seeing how many related words you know: e.g. *cocina* – kitchen, cooking or cooker; *cocer* – to cook; *cocción* – (process of) cooking; *cocinar* – to cook; *cocinero/a* – cook/chef. You can browse this section of a dictionary for further related words, or work with a friend to see who can find the most words. You can also see how many words you can find associated by ideas: *cocina – gas – eléctrico – electricidad – luz – alumbrar* etc. or by opposites: *empezar – terminar, permitir – prohibir.* The exercises at the end of the theme-based sections will help you enlarge your vocabulary, e.g. by finding cognates, synonyms and antonyms.

Websites

For links (*enlaces*), Google and Yahoo are perfectly adequate: type in **www.google.es** or **www.yahoo.es**.

All the main Spanish and Spanish American press publications have their own websites, with many features relevant to the topics covered in this book. The main publications are listed below.

Newspapers

- *El País* **www.elpais.es**
- *ABC* **www.abc.es**

- *El Mundo* **www.elmundo.es**
- *La Vanguardia* **www.lavanguardia.es**

Regional papers in the *Diario* series, e.g.:

- *Diario montañés* (Cantabria) **www.eldiariomontanes.es**

Magazines

- *Cambio16* **www.cambio16.com**
- *Tiempo* **www.tiempodehoy.com**
- *¡Hola!* **www.hola.com**
- *Marca* **www.marca.com**
- *as* **https://as.com**

You can also find a comprehensive list of publications by visiting **www.prensaescrita.com** and then typing in the relevant area after adding a slash.

For Hispanic culture in general, the *Instituto Cervantes* website is useful: **https://cvc.cervantes.es**

Other general websites with many useful links are the relevant Spanish government ministries:

- Agricultura y Pesca, Alimentación y Medio ambiente **www.mpama.gob.es**
- Asunto Exteriores y Cooperación **www.exteriores.gob.es**
- Economía, Industria y Competividad **www.mineco.gob.es**
- Empleo y Seguridad Social **www.empleo.gob.es**
- Educación, Cultura y Deporte **www.mecd.gob.es/portada-mecd**
- Energía, Turismo y Agenda Digital **www.minetad.gob.es**
- Fomento **www.fomento.gob.es**
- Hacienda y Función Pública **www.minhafp.gob.es**
- Justicia **www.mjusticia.gob.es**
- Sanidad, Servicios Sociales e Igualdad Interior **www.interior.gob.es**

The country suffixes for sites in Spanish-speaking countries are:

Argentina	.ar	Nicaragua	.ni
Bolivia	.bo	Panamá	.pa
Chile	.cl	Paraguay	.py
Colombia	.co	Perú	.pe
Costa Rica	.cr	República Dominicana	.do
Cuba	.cu	El Salvador	.sv
Ecuador	.ec	Spain	.es
Guatemala	.gt	Uruguay	.uy
México	.mx	Venezuela	.ve

For example, the Peruvian ministry of education site is **www.minedu.gob.pe**. You will find a list of possible websites for further research at the end of most of the theme-based chapters in this book.

Sección A Quiero decir...

The purpose of this section is to provide the vocabulary to enable you to state, develop and conclude a written or spoken argument. The subsections are arranged in an order that seems to be the most logical, but do remember that many words and expressions could well be used in other parts of the argument, and in other contexts.

A.1 Preparar el terreno — *Preparing the ground*

primero	first, firstly
segundo	second, secondly
tercero	third, thirdly
el tema	subject, topic, theme
el problema	problem
la crisis	crisis
la cuestión	question (for discussion), issue
en primer/segundo/tercer lugar	in the first/second/third place
al principio	at first, at the beginning
de antemano	beforehand
tenemos que preguntarnos	we have to ask ourselves
a primera vista	at first sight
a corto plazo	in the short term
a largo plazo	in the long term
ordenar los datos	to get the facts in order
despejar el terreno	to clear the ground
¿de qué se trata?	what is it about?
resumir el tema/la cuestión	to summarise the issue
afrontar el tema/la situación	to face (up to) the issue/situation
el problema que se plantea es...	the problem to be addressed/that arises is...
es un tema que ya me preocupa/interesa desde hace algún tiempo	it's a topic that has been concerning/interesting me for some time now
una crisis a escala mundial	a crisis on a world scale
una situación inquietante	a worrying situation
la preocupación predominante	the main worry/concern

A.2 Aportar más ideas — *Bringing in more ideas*

además	besides, moreover
es más	moreover

además de lo dicho	in addition to what has been said
asimismo	likewise
en principio	in principle
en esto	at this point/stage
por consiguiente por consecuencia	consequently, therefore
por otra parte	on the other hand
debido a esto	owing/due to this
de hecho	in fact
dicho de otro modo	in other words
dicho eso	that said, having said that
o sea…	or to put it another way…, or rather…
no solo… sino…	not only…but…
como ya se sabe	as we already know
es decir	that is to say, i.e.
en este contexto	in this context
por añadidura	in addition
a propósito	by the way
tanto… como…	both… and…
como resultado (de)	as a result (of)
resulta que…	it turns out that…, the result is that…
esto explica por qué…	this explains why…
no me explico por qué…	I don't understand why…
así	thus
así es que	therefore
por supuesto	of course
claro que (+ *clause*)	of course…
en realidad	in reality, in fact
aparte de eso	apart from that
se trata de	it's a question of

A.3 Obstáculos *Obstacles*

sin embargo	however
desgraciadamente por desgracia	unfortunately
no obstante	nevertheless
a pesar de esto	in spite of this
el tropiezo	the stumbling block
sea como sea	be that as it may, that's as may be
la situación va empeorando	situation is getting worse

teniendo en cuenta el hecho de que	bearing in mind the fact that
dado que	given that

A.4 Yo creo... — *I think...*

a mi parecer	in my opinion
a mi modo de ver a mí me parece que... yo opino que...	I think that...
por mi parte	for my part
desde mi punto de vista	from my point of view
(no) estoy de acuerdo con los que...	I am (not) in agreement with those who...
estoy convencido/a de que (+ *indic*)	I am persuaded/convinced that...
no estoy convencido/a de que (+ *subj*)	I am not persuaded/convinced that...
que yo sepa	as far as I know
yo que tú/usted/ellos	if I were you/them
no estoy totalmente a favor de (+ *n or inf*)	I'm not entirely in favour of...
no estoy ni a favor ni en contra de (+ *n or inf*)	I'm neither for nor against...
no es una opinión/actitud que comparta yo	it's not an opinion/attitude which I share
aunque quisiera pensar de otra manera	although I would like to think otherwise

A.5 Otros dicen... — *Others say...*

hay quienes dicen que...	there are those who say that...
la gente piensa que...	people think that...
otros constatan que...	others maintain that...
la (gran) mayoría opina que...	the (vast) majority think that...
según se oye/se lee	according to what one hears/reads
según una encuesta	according to a survey/opinion poll
sondear las opiniones	to sound out opinions
la verdad lisa y llana es...	the plain truth of the matter is...
cualquiera es capaz de ver que...	anyone can see that...
desde el punto de vista ajeno	from other people's point of view
es de presumir que... según cabe presumir	presumably
las cifras atestan que...	the figures prove that...
como ya se sabe	as is already known

que se sepa	as far as is known
no se puede menos de pensar que…	one cannot help thinking that…
es una ilusión creer que… (+ *subj*)	we're kidding ourselves if we believe that…
eso sería tremendamente optimista	that would be wildly optimistic
cualquiera que crea esto…	anyone who believes this…

A.6 La discusión sigue — *The discussion continues*

al contrario	on the contrary, on the other hand
visto así	seen like that
por un lado	on the one hand
por otro lado	on the other hand
de todos modos de todas maneras/formas	in any case, anyway
en lo que concierne en cuanto a	as for
en lugar de eso	instead of that
mientras que	whereas
no cabe duda de que…	there is no doubt that…
no se puede negar que…	there is no denying that…
es cierto que…	it's true/certain that…
el quid de la cuestión (es que…)	the crux of the matter (is that…)
hay que tener en cuenta (que…)	you have to bear in mind (that…)
me limito a señalar…	I confine myself to pointing out…
más vale… que…	it's better to…than…
vale considerar…	it's worth considering…
según toda probabilidad	in all probability
nadie ignora que…	everybody knows that…, nobody is unaware that…
por si acaso	just in case
no hay manera de saber si…	there is no way of knowing whether…
para colmo	to cap it all
y por si eso fuera poco	and as if that were not enough
no hay manera de saber si…	there is no way of knowing whether…
a juzgar por…	to judge by…, judging by…
en función de…	in proportion to…, according to (in that sense)…
en razón de…	by reason of…, because of…, due to…

A.7 Por ejemplo — *For example*

consideremos	let's consider
pongamos por caso lo de...	let's take for example the matter of...
en concreto	in particular
según el caso	as the case may be
para ilustrar el problema	to illustrate the problem
con respecto a...	with regard to...
vamos a abordar otro aspecto	let us tackle another aspect
vamos a profundizar	let's think about it in greater depth
vale agregar que...	it's worth adding that...

A.8 ¿Cómo? — *How?*

¿hasta qué punto?	to what extent?
hasta cierto punto	to a certain extent
extremadamente	extremely
totalmente	completely, utterly
principalmente	mainly, principally
tanto más	all the more so
de cierto modo de cierta manera/forma	in a certain way
de ningún modo de ninguna manera	in no way
de un modo u otro de una manera u otra	in one way or another
apenas	hardly
en ninguna circunstancia	in no circumstance(s)
simplemente sencillamente	simply
puramente	purely, merely
prácticamente	practically, nearly
parcialmente	partially, partly
igualmente	equally, to the same extent
efectivamente	actually, in fact
parecido a... similar a...	like..., similar to...
por la mayor parte	for the most part, mostly
a cambio de...	in exchange for...
se trata de saber cómo...	it's a question of knowing how...

A.9 ¿Cuándo? *When?*

durante estos últimos años/meses	in the last few years/months
hace poco	a short time/while ago
anteriormente	formerly
recientemente	recently
recién construido	recently/newly built
recién nacido	recently/newly born (*recién* can be used with various past participles in this sense)
en el momento en (el) que…	at the moment when…
en aquel mismo momento	at that very moment
en un momento dado	at a given moment
hoy (en) día	nowadays
en la actualidad	nowadays, at the present time
la situación actual	the present/current situation
mientras tanto	meanwhile, in the meantime
posteriormente con posterioridad	subsequently, afterwards
cuanto antes lo más pronto posible	as soon as possible
dentro de unos pocos días	in a few days' time
dentro de poco	soon, in a short time
sin demora	without delay
algún día	some day
desde ahora	from now (on)
a partir de este/ese momento	from this/that moment (on)
a continuación	then, next, below (on page or in list)
desde… hasta…	from…until…
nunca más	never again
en la Edad Media	in the Middle Ages
en la época de la dictadura	at the time of the dictatorship
la década	decade
durante los años noventa	during the 1990s
al final del siglo	at the turn of the century
tardar (mucho) tiempo en (+ *inf*)	to take a (very) long time in (*verb*-ing)
cada cuando	every so often
cada pocos días	every few days
a cualquier hora	at any time
por primera/segunda/última vez	for the first/second/last time
por enésima vez	for the umpteenth time
cada vez (que…)	each/every time (that…), whenever

A.10 ¿Por qué? — *Why?*

preguntarse por qué	to wonder why
deberíamos preguntarnos si…	we should ask ourselves if/whether…
según los datos	according to the facts
eso explica por qué…	that explains why…
no me explico por qué…	I can't explain/don't understand why…
se trata de saber por qué…	it's a question of knowing why…
debemos tratar de descubrir por qué…	we must try to find out why…
¿para qué?	what for?, for what purpose?
para comprender mejor	in order to understand better
puesto que… / ya que…	since/because…
por cualquier razón	for whatever reason
la razón principal	the main reason
la piedra clave	the keystone, the keynote

A.11 La verdad es que… — *The truth is that…*

The expressions followed by *que* in this section all express fact or assumed fact, and are therefore followed by the indicative.

claro que es verdad que…	of course it's true that…
lo cierto es que…	what is certain is that…
no cabe duda de que…	there's no doubt that…
en efecto yo diría que…	in fact I'd say that…
quiero dejar muy claro que…	I want to make it very clear that…
el caso es que…	the fact is that…
otro factor es que…	another factor is that…
no se puede negar que…	it cannot be denied that…
parece ser que…	it seems that…
debemos tener en cuenta que…	we have to bear in mind that…
si nos damos cuenta de que…	if we realise that…
resulta que…	the result is/it turns out that…
de ahí que…	that's the reason why…
el dilema es que…	the dilemma is that…
actualmente se calcula que…	at the moment it is estimated/ calculated that…
un 70% de los entrevistados opina que…	70% of those interviewed reckon that…
hay quienes afirman que…	there are those who maintain that…
ser consciente de que…	to be conscious/aware that…
menos mal que…	it's a good job/thank goodness that…

A.12 A mi juicio... *In my judgement...*

When the phrase makes a judgement or indicates a purpose, the verb which follows *que* is in the subjunctive. Remember that the tense of the subjunctive will depend on the rules of tense sequence, and therefore phrases containing *sería*, which is conditional, will require the imperfect subjunctive. These are marked with an asterisk (*).

a mí me parece lógico que...	it seems logical/sensible to me that...
no me sorprende que...	I'm not surprised that...
todo esto justifica que...	all this justifies (the fact) that...
parece inverosímil que...	it seems unlikely that...
parece mentira que...	it seems incredible that...
a mí me resulta curioso que...	I find it extraordinary that...
más vale que...	it's better/best that...
a mí no me importa que...	it's of no concern to me whether/that, it doesn't matter to me whether/that...
no es porque...	it's not because...
¿no parece significativo que...?	doesn't it seem significant that...?
esto explica que se escriba así...	that explains why it should be written like that...
es intolerable/insoportable que...	it's intolerable that...
me preocupa bastante que...	I'm somewhat/rather worried that...
¿por qué tenemos que soportar que...?	why should we put up with the fact that...?
sería un milagro que...*	it would be a miracle if...
mi preferencia sería que...*	my preference would be that...
¿no sería mejor que...?*	wouldn't it be better if...?
si no fuera porque...*	if it weren't for the fact that...
es de suma importancia que...	it is of extreme importance that...
¿por qué no exigimos todos que...?	why don't we all demand that...?
es de lamentar que...	it is to be regretted that...
es una vergüenza nacional que...	it's a national disgrace that...
es incluso más sorprendente que...	it's even more astonishing that...
lo fundamental debe ser que...	the main thing should be that...
pongamos por caso que...	let's suppose that...

A.13 La validez del argumento *The validity of the argument*

razonar	to reason
el razonamiento	the reasoning
un caso irrebatible	a watertight case
un argumento de peso	a strong/robust argument
este modo de enfocar la cuestión	this approach to the question

si aceptamos este punto de vista	if we accept this point of view
el argumento no vale, porque…	the argument is no good, because…
rechazar un argumento	to reject an argument
condenar rotundamente	to condemn roundly
ver/no ver lo esencial del asunto	to see/miss the point
el argumento no está bien fundado	the argument won't hold water
no tiene pies ni cabeza	it's all at sixes and sevens
carece de sentido	it lacks sense/meaning
carece de consistencia	it lacks consistency
el punto flaco del argumento	the weak point of the argument
no tiene nada que ver con la realidad	it has nothing to do with reality
hacer la vista gorda (a)	to turn a blind eye (to)
pongamos el argumento patas arriba	let's turn the argument on its head

A.14 Soluciones y conclusiones *Solutions and conclusions*

de acuerdo	agreed
(estar) de acuerdo con…	(to be) in agreement with
a fin de cuentas	after all, when all is said and done
en resumen	to sum up (*adv*), in brief
resumir	to sum up
la clave del problema tiene que ser	the key to the problem has to be
la solución que se destaca	the solution which stands out
tomar medidas urgentes	to take urgent measures
ya hemos constatado que…	we have already stated that…
teniendo en cuenta todos los puntos de vista	bearing in mind all points of view
podemos deducir que…	we can deduce that…
es una perspectiva…	the outlook is…
optimista	optimistic/bright
poco optimista	not very optimistic
(muy) pesimista	(very) pessimistic/gloomy
(nada) favorable	(not very) favourable
aunque con ciertas dudas/reservas	although with certain doubts/reservations
por fin	finally, at last
en conclusión / para concluir	in conclusion
para que la situación siga mejorando	so that the situation continues to improve
de modo que la situación no empeore	so that the situation does not deteriorate
ojalá pudiera concluir diciendo que…	I wish I could conclude by saying that…
no hay otra conclusión que valga	there is no other valid conclusion

Sección B Amigos algo falsos y muy falsos

Many Spanish words of almost identical appearance to their English equivalents also have much the same meaning. Some, however, although they may share one or more meanings, are used more commonly with a different sense, as in Section B.1. Some other words have a totally different meaning, which could even lead you into embarrassing situations. These latter, in Section B.2, are known as 'false friends'. So pay close attention to these lists!

B.1 ¡Cuidadito! *Be a bit careful!*

absolutamente	absolutely (in agreement with affirmative or negative statements)
en absoluto	not at all, absolutely not
adecuado/a	suitable
admirar	to surprise, to astonish (also 'to admire')
agitar	to wave (arms etc.)
aguardar	to wait (for)
alterar(se)	to make/get upset/angry
anciano/a	(applied to people) old person
antiguo/a	ancient, former
asistir (a)	to be present at, to attend (NOT 'to assist')
la asistencia	attendance (rather than 'assistance')
la batería	drums (in band), drummer (also 'battery')
bruto/a	coarse, rough, uncouth; gross (weight etc.)
la cacerola	saucepan
el/la canguro	baby-sitter
la comisión	committee
la comodidad	comfort
completo/a	full (hotel, bus etc.) (also 'complete')
la conferencia	lecture, talk (also 'conference')
el cristal	pane of glass, window pane
crudo/a	raw, uncooked, untreated
la cuestión	question (to be discussed, rather than asked)
la desgracia	misfortune, bad luck
por desgracia	unfortunately
divertir(se)	to amuse/be amused
efectivamente en efecto	in fact, indeed, actually
la época	period of time, season, era

fatal	dreadful, awful, ghastly
genial	inspired, brilliant
el genio	disposition, nature; bad temper
ignorar	not to know, to be ignorant of
el/la infante/a	prince/princess
la memoria	memory (mechanism)
la moneda	coin; currency
particular	private
la ración	portion, helping (of food)
real	royal (also 'real', 'true')
el régimen (*pl* los regímenes)	diet (also 'regime')
registrar	to search, to inspect (baggage etc.)
regular (*adj*)	so-so (health, quality etc.)
solicitar	to ask for, to request; to apply for (job)
suceder	to happen (only 'succeed' in sense of 'come after')

B.2 ¡Mucho cuidado! *Be very careful!*

acomodar(se)	to make (oneself) comfortable
acostar(se)	to put/go to bed, to lie down
actual	present (in time)
actualmente	at present, now
afrontar	to face up to
avisar	to warn
la bala	bullet
balancear(se)	to rock, to sway
el balón	(large) ball, e.g. football
bizarro/a	brave, gallant
el campo	field; country (as opposed to town)
la carpeta	folder, portfolio
casual	chance (*adj*)
casualmente por casualidad	by chance
la casualidad	chance, coincidence
el c(h)rismas	Christmas card
el collar	necklace
el compromiso	commitment, engagement; predicament
comprometerse	to commit oneself; to get into a predicament
concretar(se)	to make/become more specific
el delito	crime, offence

el disgusto	annoyance, displeasure
embarazarse	to become pregnant
embarazada	pregnant
energético/a (*adj*)	to do with energy, e.g. *la crisis energética* (use *enérgico/a* for person etc.)
eventual	fortuitous, dependent upon circumstances
el éxito	success
fastidiar(se)	to annoy, to get annoyed
el fastidio	annoyance
la gana	desire, wish
tener ganas de	to wish to, to feel like (doing sth)
gentil	elegant, graceful
el gusto	pleasure, delight; taste
honesto/a	decent, chaste
honrado/a	honest, honourable
el idioma	language
jubilarse	to retire
largo/a	long
la letra	letter of alphabet; handwriting; words of song
loco/a	mad
molestar	to annoy, to irritate
la molestia	annoyance, irritation
el nudo	knot
el obsequio	gift, present
la parcela	plot of land
el pariente/la parienta	relative, relation
pinchar	to prick, to puncture
pisar	to tread, to trample
el preservativo	condom
pretender	to seek to, to try to; to claim
quitar(se)	to take away, to remove, to take off
el rato	(short) while
recordar	to remember
el refrán	proverb, saying
la renta	income
revolver	to stir, to mix up, to turn round/over
la ropa	clothes
sano/a	healthy
el talón	heel (of shoe); cheque, cheque stub
la tinta	ink; dye
la tormenta	storm

Sección C ¡Escoge la palabra correcta!

You need to take great care when selecting the Spanish equivalent of these English words.

C.1 ¡Cuidado! *Careful!*

to appear	
come into sight	aparecer
seem	parecer
to apply	
for job	solicitar, pedir
substance (to)	aplicar (a)
to argue	
quarrel	reñir
reason	argüir
to ask	
a question	preguntar
sb for sth	pedir algo a alguien
sb to do sth	pedir a alguien que haga algo
to become	
+ noun	hacerse, convertirse en
+ occupation	hacerse, llegar a ser
+ adjective	ponerse; hacerse (*implies effort*)
or make verb from adjective	e.g. independizarse (*become independent*)
both	
referring to two people or objects	ambos/as, los/las dos
both…and…	tanto… como…
to burn	
consume or damage by fire	quemar
be on fire	arder
to care	
look after	cuidar
care/worry about	preocuparse por, interesarse por
take care	tener cuidado

care (*n*)

anxiety	**la inquietud**

to come	**venir**
for 'come in/out/up/down' etc. see also under 'go'.	

to drive

drive a vehicle	**conducir**
drive somewhere	**ir en coche**
drive + *adj*	**volver (e.g. volver loco/a – *drive mad*)**

to enjoy

have use/benefit of (circumstances, health etc.)	**gozar**
take delight in	**gustar (e.g. ¿Te gustó la película? – *Did you enjoy the film?*)**
enjoy oneself	**divertirse, pasarlo bien**

to fail

be a flop, not succeed	**fracasar**
crops, machinery etc.	**fallar**
in obligation, duty etc.	**faltar**
an exam	**suspender**
fail to do sth	**dejar de hacer algo**

There are numerous other idiomatic uses: check in the dictionary.

to get

obtain	**obtener, conseguir**
receive	**recibir**
become + *adj*	**ponerse**
followed by an adjective in English translation of certain reflexive verbs	**cansarse (*to get tired*); mojarse (*to get wet*)**
go and get	**ir por**

This is a multipurpose word in English. The best tip is to find another English word which expresses the meaning of 'get' and use the Spanish equivalent.

to go	**ir**
go/come in(to)	**entrar (en)**
go/come out (of)	**salir (de)**
go/come up	**subir**
go/come down	**bajar**
go/come across	**cruzar, atravesar**

go/come back	**volver**
go/come by	**pasar**
go away	**irse, marcharse, alejarse**

See also Section C.2.3 below.

to know	
know a fact, know that…	**saber (que)**
know how to	**saber +** ***inf***
know/be acquainted with a person/place	**conocer**
NOT to know (a fact/that…)	**ignorar**

last	
in series	**último/a**
previous (e.g. last Monday)	**pasado/a**

to leave	
go off/away	**irse, marcharse**
train, plane etc.	**salir (de)**
leave (the house, work etc.)	**salir (de casa, del trabajo, etc.)**
allow to remain	**dejar**
abandon	**abandonar**

to let	
rent out	**alquilar**
permit, let sth happen	**dejar (+** ***inf or subj*****), permitir (+** ***subj*****), que +** ***pres subj***

to love	
a person	**querer, amar**
an activity, food etc.	**encantar (e.g. me encanta –** ***I love it*****)**
fall in love (with)	**enamorarse (de)**
be in love (with)	**estar enamorado/a (de)**

to look	
look at	**mirar**
look for, have a look for	**buscar**
seem	**parecer**
look like, resemble	**parecerse a**

look (*n*)	
act of looking	**la mirada**
appearance	**el aspecto**
fashion	**la moda, el estilo**

to manage

manage to	conseguir, lograr + *inf*
a company	dirigir, gestionar

to move

general	mover (*trans*), moverse (*intrans*)
move house	mudarse de casa

to order

command	mandar, ordenar
request (e.g. purchase)	pedir, encargar
in restaurant	pedir

order (*n*)

for purchase or food	el pedido
command	la orden
succession, arrangement	el orden

to put

general	poner
place	colocar
put into	meter (en)

quite

completely	totalmente, completamente
rather, somewhat	bastante, algo, un poco
not quite	no del todo

to reflect

reflect light	reflejar
think	reflexionar

to run

action of running	correr
run an organisation etc.	dirigir
in a particular direction:	
run up	subir corriendo
run down	bajar corriendo
run in(to)	entrar corriendo (en)
run out (from)	salir corriendo (de)

to sit

sit down (i.e. action)	sentarse
be sitting/seated (state)	estar sentado/a

sorry

when you interrupt or unintentionally hurt sb	¡perdón!
to apologise emphatically, generally express regret, be sorry about	sentir, lamentar
to be (very) sorry that…	sentir (mucho) que + *subj*

to stand

stand up	levantarse, ponerse de pie
be standing (if bodily position is of importance)	estar de pie
be standing (if bodily position is not important)	estar parado
tolerate, put up with	aguantar, soportar

to stop

bring/come to a halt	parar(se), detener(se)
stop doing sth	dejar/terminar de hacer algo
cease, e.g. rain	cesar
prevent sb from doing sth	impedir que alguien haga algo

to succeed

be successful	tener éxito
succeed in (doing)	conseguir/lograr + *inf*
be next in succession to	suceder a

to take

general	tomar
take hold of, catch	coger Warning: this verb has vulgar sexual connotations in most of Spanish America – use *tomar.*
occupy	ocupar
take sb or sth somewhere, i.e. lead, transport	llevar
take out (from)	sacar (de)

then

next	luego, después
at that time	entonces
so, in that case	pues, entonces

time

concept or duration	el tiempo
occasion	la vez
time of day	la hora
period/span of time	la época
short period of time/while	el rato
to have a good time	divertirse, pasarlo bien

to try

endeavour to	tratar de, intentar, procurar
try out, try on (i.e. test, sample)	probar

to turn (*as intrans v*)

revolve	girar
change direction	volver
turn round	volverse, dar la vuelta
turn into (become)	convertirse en, transformarse en
turn + *adj*	volverse, ponerse

to walk

action of walking	andar
to go for a walk	pasearse, dar un paseo
in a particular direction:	
walk up	subir andando
walk down	bajar andando
walk in(to)	entrar andando (en)
walk out (of)	salir andando (de)

to wipe

clean	limpiar
dry	secar, enjugar

to work

do work	trabajar
function	funcionar

work (*n*)

job, the work you do	el trabajo
work of art	la obra
road/building works	las obras

C.2 Sinónimos para palabras corrientes — *Synonyms for common words*

We are all inclined to use common, general-purpose words such as 'to be', 'to have', 'lots of', when we could and should be more precise. Here are some alternative suggestions. However, a word of warning: some 'synonyms' might not be synonymous with all meanings of a particular word, and might have a particular nuance, hence the reason for including some examples to help you decide.

C.2.1 Ser/Estar — *To be*

Be aware first of all of the differences between ***ser*** and ***estar***, which you will find fully explained in any grammar book.

Estar

- be in a place, position or state (talking of people): ***encontrarse***, ***hallarse***

Loli se encontraba enferma aquel día.	Loli was ill that day.

- be in a place, talking of objects or towns, cities etc: ***encontrarse***, ***hallarse***, ***situarse***, and rather more sophisticatedly, ***ubicarse***

Salamanca se encuentra ubicada/se sitúa/se ubica en el río Tormes.	Salamanca is on the river Tormes.

- be in a state, usually after an action (not necessarily expressed): ***quedar***

La ciudad quedaba en ruinas.	The town was (left) in ruins.

Ser

- be considered: ***considerarse***

Pepe se considera muy listo	Pepe thinks he is very clever

C.2.2 Hay — *There is/are*

- ***se encuentra(n)***: there is/are to be found
- ***se ve(n)***: there is/are to be seen

Se encuentran/ven muchos edificios históricos en esta ciudad.	There are lots of historic buildings in this town.

C.2.3 Ir, etc. — *To go/come*

- to a place: ***dirigirse a***, ***viajar***, ***desplazarse a*** (implies effort or travel)

Viajo/Me desplazo cada día desde Segovia a Madrid.	I go/come from Segovia to Madrid each day.

- go away: ***irse***, but also ***marcharse***

¿Cuándo te marchas/te vas?	When are you going (away)?

- go/move away: ***alejarse*** (tends to emphasise increasing distance; it's derived from *lejos*)

El tren se alejaba de la estación.	The train was going/moving away from the station.

- go/come towards, approach: ***acercarse***, ***aproximarse*** (often but not necessarily more abstract)

El tren se acercaba.	The train was coming/approaching.
Se aproxima el invierno.	Winter is coming.

C.2.4 Mucho/mucha/muchos/muchas — *A lot, much, lots, many*

- Try also:

(una) gran cantidad de	a large quantity of
una cantidad enorme de	a huge/vast quantity of
grandes cantidades de	large quantities of
un montón de/montones de	a heap of, heaps of (slightly more colloquial)
una multitud de	a multitude/masses of
una muchedumbre de	a great number of
un sinnúmero de	no end of, a great many
miles/millares de	thousands of
toneladas de	tons of

C.2.5 Muy — *Very*

- You can often use the suffix ***-ísimo*** on an adjective:

caro – carísimo	very/extremely expensive
rico – riquísimo	very/extremely rich

- Use:

extremadamente: extremadamente generoso	extremely generous
enormemente: enormemente feo	enormously ugly

and other adverbs which suggest an extreme or superlative: *importantemente*, *notablemente*, etc.

Sección D El cine y la literatura

Vocabulario clave	*Key vocabulary*
el género	genre
la ambientación	setting
el personaje	character
la trama	plot
el tema	theme
la técnica	technique, method
el estilo	style
la obra	work, œuvre
la película el film(e)	film
la novela	novel
el relato	story
la historia	history, story
la obra de teatro la obra dramática/teatral	play
el drama	drama
el poema	poem
la poesía	poetry, poem
el suceso	event, episode
el/la cineasta	film-maker
el/la escritor(a)	writer
el/la autor(a)	author
el/la novelista	novelist
el/la dramaturgo/a	playwright
el poeta/la poetisa	poet
el director(a)	director
el actor/la actriz	actor/actress
la actuación	acting, performance
el rol el papel	role
contar relatar	to tell, to relate
actuar	to act

En general	***In general***
la acogida del público	reception of the audience
el/la apasionado/a de la ciencia-ficción	science-fiction addict
la biblioteca	library
el/la bibliotecario/a	librarian
la característica el rasgo	feature
el efecto	effect
desgarrador(a)	heart-breaking
el/la editor(a)	editor
el ejemplar la copia	copy of book
la (casa) editorial	publishing house
emocionante	exciting, emotional
el estreno	first showing/performance
estrenar una película/una obra	to put on a film/play for the first time
fascinar	to fascinate
fascinante	fascinating
la fuerza expresiva	expressive force
gozar del cine/teatro	to enjoy the cinema/theatre
la ilusión	excitement
impactante	striking
inspirarse en	to be inspired by
el/la lector(a)	reader
la lectura	reading
la librería	bookshop
el/la librero/a	bookseller
la localidad	seat
a lo largo de su carrera	throughout his/her career
ofrecer una visión	to offer a vision
el realismo	realism
redactar	to write, to edit
relatar	to recount, to narrate
la representación	performance, show
la reseña	review
el resumen	summary
la sátira	satire
la secuela	sequel
la sinópsis	synopsis
el soliloquio	soliloquy

la taquilla	box office
el telón de fondo	backdrop
en toda su obra	in the whole of his/her work
una trilogía	a trilogy
la vestimenta	clothing
el vestuario	wardrobe, costumes

El cine	***Cinema***
la pantalla	screen
la estrella de cine	film star
rodar una película	to shoot a film
el guión	script
el/la guionista	scriptwriter
el largometraje	full-length film, feature film
el cortometraje	short (film)
doblar en castellano	to dub into Spanish
la banda sonora	sound track
los subtítulos	subtitles
la película está subtitulada en catalán	the film is subtitled in Catalan
para todos los públicos	suitable for all ages
no recomendada a menores de [x] años	not suitable for those under [x] years of age
la sesión continua	continuous performance
el plató de cine	film set
el rodaje	filming
apareció en su primer largometraje	[he/she] appeared in his/her first feature film
estrenarse una película	to premiere a film
la película emociona desde el primer momento	the film is thrilling from the first moment
un cineasta creativo	a creative film-maker
la voz en off	voice-over
pasar a la historia del cine	to go down in cinematic history
la película está basada en…	the film is based on…
el séptimo arte	cinema
una película biográfica	a biopic
romper con el cine convencional	to break away from conventional cinema
la representación de un filme/una película	showing of a film

La novela	***The novel***
el libro de bolsillo	paperback
el cuento	short story, tale
el/la cuentista	short story writer
la (auto)biografía	(auto)biography
(auto)biográfico/a	(auto)biographical
la crónica	chronicle
el capítulo	chapter
saber contar una historia	to know how to tell a story, to be a good storyteller
el cuento alcanza su desenlace	the story unfolds
el/la escritor(a) de vanguardia	avant-garde writer
disfrutar de una buena lectura	to enjoy a good read
enriquecer el relato	to make the story richer
al comienzo/al final de la novela	at the beginning/end of the novel

El teatro	***Theatre***
la obra dramática/teatral	play
poner una obra en escena	to produce a play
la puesta en escena	production
los personajes de un drama	characters in a play
interpretar una obra teatral	to perform/interpret a play
la representación de una obra dramática	performance of a play
el espectáculo teatral	(theatre) show
el acto	act
la escena el escenario	stage, scene
el montaje	design, décor
una obra ambientada en Barcelona	a play set in Barcelona
al caer el telón	when the curtain falls/fell
aplaudir	to applaud
los aplausos	applause
silbar	to hiss, to boo
ante el público	in front of the audience
el miedo a salir a la escena	stage fright
el maquillaje	make-up
maquillarse	to put one's make-up on
el teatro callejero	street theatre
los títeres	puppets
la temporada	season (theatre etc.)

el decorado de teatro	theatre set
estrenarse una obra de teatro	to premiere, to perform a play for the first time

La poesía	***Poetry***
la obra poética	poetic work
el verso	line; verse
la estrofa	verse, stanza
rimar	to rhyme
el ritmo	rhythm
embellecer el lenguaje	to embellish the language
el estado de ánimo del poeta	the poet's state of mind
la primera/segunda, etc. estrofa	first/second etc. stanza
el sentido figurado	figurative sense
el uso de la metáfora/del símil	use of metaphor/simile

El contexto	***Context***
el medio ambiente el entorno	environment
describir/mostrar el entorno/el medio ambiente	to describe/show the environment
el ambiente de la aldea, del barrio, etc.	atmosphere of the village, district etc.
la ambientación de una novela/una película	setting, atmosphere of a novel/film
ambientar una película en…	to set a film in…
suceder en el pasado/presente/futuro	to take place in the past/present/future
un sentido de lugar	a sense of place
transmitir la impresión de un lugar	to convey the impression of a place
el marco histórico/social	historical/social background
recrear el período/la época	to re-create the period/era
escenificado/a en un periodo clave	set in a key period
el lugar donde se representa la obra	the place where the work is being performed
localizar la novela/el filme en Buenos Aires	to set the novel/film in Buenos Aires
la trama refleja la época	the plot reflects the era
reflejar la realidad de la vida de…	to reflect the reality of the life of…
el paisaje urbano/agrario	urban/country landscape
la acción está basada en hecho reales	the action is based on real events
el mundo imaginario	imaginary world
reconocer de inmediato	to recognise immediately
realista	realist(ic)

El argumento/La trama	***Plot***
el subtema	sub-plot
el resumen del argumento	plot summary
la secuencia de los sucesos	sequence of events
el desarrollo de la trama/intriga	plot development
la complejidad del argumento	complexity of the plot
las fases del desarrollo	phases of development
una trama muy enrevesada	a very involved plot
a lo largo del relato	as the story progresses
una escena emocionante	an exciting/emotional scene
el desenlace	outcome, dénouement
tener un desenlace trágico	to have a tragic denouement/ending
al final de la novela/película	at the end of the novel/film

Los temas	***Themes***
el tema clave	key theme
presentar un tema	to present a theme
desarrollar el tema	to develop the theme
un tema actual	a current theme/issue
el tema controvertido	controversial theme
el tema secundario	secondary theme
la historia agridulce de amor	bitter-sweet love story
la relevancia de los temas tratados	the relevance of the themes dealt with
subrayar el mensaje	to highlight the message
se trata del amor/de la fantasía, etc.	it's a question of love/fantasy etc.

Los personajes	***Characters***
destaca el personaje (x)	character (x) stands out
un personaje inolvidable	an unforgettable character
el/la protagonista el papel principal	main role, protagonist
el/la antagonista	antagonist
el actor/la actriz principal	lead actor/actress
el personaje secundario	secondary/supporting character
tener una personalidad dura/simpática/alegre	to have a hard/kind/cheerful personality
la vida interior de los personajes	the characters' inner life
el desarrollo psicológico	psychological development
el desarrollo de un conflicto entre…	the development of a conflict between…
el personaje reacciona a…	the character reacts to…
[x] es caracterizado/a por…	[x] is characterised by…

el desarrollo del personaje la evolución del personaje	the development of the character
diferenciarse mucho en su personalidad	to differ greatly in their personality
parecerse mucho	to look very alike
ser parecido/a a	to be similar to
tener rasgos semejantes	to have similar features
llevarse bien/mal	to get on well/badly
una relacion dominada por…	a relationship dominated by…
el físico de un personaje	a character's appearance
identificarse totalmente con el protagonista	to identify fully with the main character
el grupo en el que se basa el relato	the group on whom the story is based
La actuación	***Performance***
hacer un papel desempeñar un papel	to play a part/role
interpretar un papel	to interpret, to play a role
la interpretación de un papel	interpretation of/performance in a part
la malinterpretación	misinterpretation
protagonizar	to star in
una película/obra protagonizada por [x]	a film/play with [x] in the leading role
el reparto de una obra dramática/película	cast of a play/film
dar vida a un personaje	to bring a character to life
retratar a un personaje	to portray a character
el retrato	portrait
La técnica	***Technique, method***
el motivo recurrente	recurring/recurrent motif
la complejidad estructural	structural complexity
presagiar	to foreshadow
la escena retrospectiva	flashback
el salto en el tiempo	jump in time
el desarrollo lineal	linear development
ir en orden cronológico	to go in chronological order
un giro inesperado	an unexpected twist
entrelazar las historias	to interweave the stories
hilvanar un relato	to join (parts of) a story together
mezclar la realidad con la fantasía	to mix real world and fantasy

crear tensión	to create tension
mantener en vilo	to keep in suspense
el suspense (*Sp*)/suspenso (*LAm*)	suspense
el tono	tone
magistral	masterly
el registro coloquial	colloquial register/speech
la imaginería	imagery
la imagen visual/táctil/auditiva/ sensorial	visual/tactile/auditory/sensory image
una imagen eficaz	an effective image
el diálogo realista	realistic dialogue
tener un estilo innovador	to have an innovative style
el uso del lenguaje	use of language
La técnica cinematográfica	***Cinematic technique***
la escenografía	setting, *mise-en-scène*
la cámara	camera
congelar una imagen	to freeze an image
el plano medio	medium shot
el plano general	long/wide-angle shot
en primer plano	close-up
el ángulo bajo	low-angle
el travelling	tracking shot
a corta distancia	close range
hacer un paneo	to pan out
los efectos especiales	special effects
el corte	cut
fundirse	to fade (image)
el fundido	fade
La técnica narrativa	***Narrative technique***
el narrador relata la historia	the narrator tells the story
la narrativa	narrative
la narración en primera/tercera persona	first-/third-person narration
el narrador omnisciente	omniscient narrator
el punto de vista	point of view
la estructura de una novela	structure of a novel
la expresión	phrasing, expression
la descripción del vestuario	description of clothing
el ritmo narrativo	narrative rhythm/pacing
la destreza del autor/de la autora	the author's skill

el realismo mágico	magical realism
el lenguaje literario	literary language
la metáfora	metaphor
la alegoría	allegory
la hipérbole	hyperbole
emplear un lenguaje figurativo	to use figurative language

La técnica teatral	***Technique in the theatre***
escenificar	to dramatise, to stage
la escenificación	staging, dramatisation
el planteamiento	exposition (of plot)
el nudo	central part of play
el desenlace del drama	denouement of the play
la catarsis	catharsis
la unidad de tiempo/acción/lugar	unity of time/action/place
la acotación	stage direction
el uso del coro	use of the chorus
el diálogo teatral	theatre dialogue

Los géneros cinematográficos	***Types of films***
el dibujo animado	cartoon
la película de acción	action film
la película de ciencia ficción	sci-fi film
la comedia	comedy
el documental	documentary
la película de espionaje	spy film
la película bélica	war film
la película musical	musical
la película romántica	romantic film
la película de suspense (*Sp*)/suspenso (*LAm*)	thriller
la película de terror	horror film

Los géneros novelísticos	***Novelistic genres***
la novela de aventuras	adventure novel
la novela de ciencia ficción	science-fiction novel
la novela de crimen	crime novel
la novela por entregas	serial
la novela de espionaje	spy novel
la novela gótica	Gothic novel
la novela histórica	historical novel
la novela negra/de intriga	thriller

la novela policíaca	detective novel
la novela rosa	romantic novel
el relato breve	short story
Los géneros teatrales	***Theatrical genres***
la comedia de costumbres	comedy of manners
la farsa	farce
el melodrama	melodrama
la ópera	opera
la tragedia	tragedy
la zarzuela	Spanish musical comedy
Los géneros poéticos	***Poetic genres***
la poesía épica	epic poetry
la poesía dramática	dramatic poetry
la poesía lírica	lyric poetry
El éxito	***Success***
tener éxito	to be successful
premiado/a	prize-winning
el galardón	award, prize
el Óscar	Oscar
el Goya	Goya (Spanish film award)
brillar	to shine
la película [española] más taquillera de la historia	the biggest box-office hit in the history of [Spanish] cinema
un éxito arrollador	a resounding success
el premio literario	literary prize/award
la editorial	publisher
las ventas de libros	book sales
la feria del libro	book fair
estar entre los libros más vendidos	to be among the best-selling books
el premio Nobel de literatura	Nobel Prize for literature
la tirada	edition, print run
el máximo logro	greatest achievement

Websites

www.alohacriticon.com/cine

https://elpais.com/diario/2000/12/05/cultura/975970804_850215.html (https://tinyurl.com/ybqsprpp)

www.spanisharts.com

Theme 1

The evolution of Spanish society

1 El cambio en la estructura familiar

Los cambios en la familia — *Changes in the family*

Vocabulario clave	***Key vocabulary***
los padres los progenitores	parents
criar una familia	to bring up/raise a family
los lazos familiares	family ties
la institución familiar	the institution of the family
convivir	to live together
la pareja	couple; partner
el hogar	home
la casa familiar	family home
el entorno familiar	family environment

Tipos de familias	***Types of family***
la familia de acogida	foster family
la familia de raza mixta	mixed-race family
la familia disfuncional	disfunctional family
la familia ensamblada	patchwork/blended family
la familia extensa	extended family
la familia homoparental	family with same-sex parents
la familia monoparental	single-parent family
la familia nuclear	nuclear family
una familia poco convencional	an unconventional family
la familia tradicional	traditional family
una familia unida	a close family

La familia extensa/extendida	***The extended family***
el/la abuelo/a	grandfather/-mother
los abuelos	grandparents
los parientes los familiares	relatives

el/la nieto/a	grandson/granddaughter
los nietos	grandchildren
el/la primo/a	cousin
el/la sobrino/a	nephew/niece
los sobrinos	nephews and nieces
el/la tío/a	uncle/aunt
los tíos	uncle(s) and aunt(s)
el parentesco	relationship, kinship

Otros parientes	***Other relatives***
la familia política	in-laws
el/la cuñado/a	brother-/sister-in-law
la nuera	daughter-in-law
el/la suegro/a	father-/mother-in-law
el yerno	son-in-law
el padrastro	stepfather
la madrastra	stepmother
la madrina	godmother
el padrino	godfather
los padrinos	godparents
el/la ahijado/a	godson/daughter
el/la hermanastro/a el/la hermano/a de leche	half (or foster)-brother/sister

Unos grandes cambios en la familia	***Some major changes in the family***
los cambios sociales acelerados	rapid social change
los cambios radicales en la familia	radical changes in the family
los cambios legislativos	changes in the law
el declive de la familia tradicional	the decline of the traditional family
la proliferación de las uniones de hecho	the proliferation of common-law relationships
la creciente diversidad de las estructuras familiares	the growing diversity of family structures
tener menos hijos	to have fewer children
el descenso de la natalidad	drop in the birth rate
tener a los hijos más tarde	to have children later

Los cambios en las relaciones / *Changes in relationships*

Vocabulario clave	*Key vocabulary*
la mujer	wife; woman
el marido	husband
el/la esposo/a	husband/wife
el/la conyuge	spouse, (married) partner
los hermanos	siblings, brother(s) and sister(s)
el padre soltero	single father/parent (male)
la madre soltera	single mother/parent (female)

Las relaciones parentales	*Parental relationships*
el cabeza de la familia	head of the family
una relación heterosexual/homosexual	a heterosexual/homosexual relationship
la orientación sexual	sexual orientation
la homosexualidad	homosexuality
el lesbianismo	lesbianism
ser gay/lesbiana	to be gay/lesbian
ser/quedarse soltero/a	to be/remain single
la unión de hecho	common-law relationship
la cohabitación	cohabitation
la maternidad	maternity
la paternidad	parenthood, fatherhood
tolerar a los demás	to tolerate others
la polémica	controversy
controvertido/a	controversial
discutir	to argue
amoroso/a	loving, affectionate
la muestra de cariño	display of affection

Otras relaciones	*Other relationships*
el/la amante	lover/mistress
la aventura	brief affair
ligar / coquetear	to flirt
el ligue	affair, fling
el devaneo	flirtation
la cita	date
la promiscuidad	promiscuity

andar en relaciones con tener relaciones con	to have an affair with
tener una relación especial con...	to have a special relationship with...
estar enamorado/a (de)	to be in love (with)
llevar una relación seria	to have a serious relationship
desarrollar una relación	to develop a relationship
la relación de pareja	partner relationship
la convivencia	living together
arrejuntarse (*col*)	to shack up together
llevar conviviendo [x años]	to have been living together for [x years]
compartir	to share
la pareja del mismo sexo	same sex couple
el/la compañero/a	partner
el/la ex cónyuge	ex-husband/-wife
comportarse	to behave
la conducta	behaviour
la liberalización de las relaciones sexuales	liberalising of sexual relationships
las citas por Internet	internet dating
buscar pareja por la Red	to look for a partner via the web
el portal de citas	dating portal
la foto de perfil	profile picture
Los abuelos	***Grandparents***
envejecer	to age, to become old
estar jubilado/a	to be retired
el asilo de ancianos	old people's home
geriátrico/a	geriatric
el cuidado de ancianos	care of the aged
el/la cuidador(a)	carer
cumplir el papel de los padres	to carry out the role of the parents
involucrarse en el cuidado de los nietos	to participate in the care of the grandchildren
recoger a los niños del colegio	to pick up the children from school
criar a un nieto	to bring up a grandchild
Los niños	***Children***
tener familia	to have a family
el nacimiento	birth
nacer	to be born
el pañal	nappy

cambiar pañales	to change nappies
criar	to bring up
los gemelos	twins (identical)
los mellizos	twins (non-identical)
conceder la adopción	to grant the right to adopt
un/una hijo/a en adopción	child for adoption
la adopción gay	gay adoption
la guardería	nursery
el/la tutor(a)	guardian
el permiso de paternidad	paternity leave
la baja por maternidad/paternidad	maternity/paternity leave
la custodia de los niños	custody of the children
ejercer la guarda	to have custody
los derechos de visita	access/visiting rights
el bienestar de los niños	the well-being of the children
las relaciones con los hijos	the relationship with the children
las obligaciones de los padres para con sus hijos	the obligations of parents towards their children
tener hijos sin estar casados	to have children without being married
la inestabilidad emocional	emotional instability
la (in)seguridad	(in)security
construir una buena relación con los hijos	to build a good relationship with children
interesarse en las actividades de los hijos	to be interested in children's activities
el respeto mutuo	mutual respect
confiar en alguien	to trust someone
comprender los sentimientos del otro	to understand another's feelings
saber distanciarse	to know how to step back
marcar límites	to set boundaries
la brecha generacional	generation gap
mantener un control demasiado rígido	to keep too rigid a control
el espacio personal	personal space
desear una libertad mayor	to want greater freedom
Un día los hijos se emancipan.	Children break free one day.
volar el nido	to fly the nest
meterse en problemas	to get into trouble
La vida sexual	***Sex life***
desear hijos	to want a family
la planificación familiar	family planning

la contracepción/anticoncepción	contraception
la píldora anticonceptiva	contraceptive pill
los métodos anticonceptivos	contraceptive/birth-control methods
el anticonceptivo	contraceptive
el preservativo / el condón	condom
el control de la natalidad	birth control
el aborto	abortion
abortar	to have an abortion/a miscarriage
el niño probeta	test-tube baby
la inseminación artificial	artificial insemination
la madre portadora	surrogate mother
la fertilidad / la fecundidad	fertility
la fecundación *in vitro* (FIV)	*in-vitro* fertilisation (IVF)
la fertilización asistida	assisted reproduction
embarazada	pregnant
un embarazo (no) deseado	a wanted (an unwanted) pregnancy
interrumpir el embarazo	to terminate the pregnancy
la libertad sexual	sexual freedom

Los cambios en el matrimonio — *Changes to marriage*

Vocabulario clave	***Key vocabulary***
casarse (con)	to get married (to)
el casamiento	wedding/marriage (ceremony or state)
el matrimonio	marriage (the state)
contraer matrimonio	to enter into matrimony/marriage
el/la prometido/a	fiancé(e)
la boda	wedding (i.e. the ceremony)
divorciarse	to get divorced
separarse	to get separated

El matrimonio	***Marriage***
la institución matrimonial	institution of marriage
prometerse (con)	to get engaged (to)
prometer	to promise
estar (com)prometido/a/os	to be engaged

el compromiso (matrimonial)	engagement to marry
emparentar con una familia	to marry into a family
el noviazgo	engagement, courtship
casarse de penalti	to have a shotgun wedding
el contrato de matrimonio	the marriage contract
estar felizmente casado/a/os	to be happily married
el matrimonio (in)feliz	(un)happy marriage
el fracaso matrimonial	marital failure
obligados a convivir	forced to live together
el asesoramiento matrimonial	marriage guidance
ayudarse uno a otro	to help each other
el apoyo mutuo	mutual support
el matrimonio homosexual/gay	gay marriage
la unión civil	civil partnership
el reconocimiento legal del matrimonio gay	legal recognition of gay marriage
mantener un hogar	to maintain a household
el acuerdo prenupcial	pre-nuptial agreement
el índice de matrimonio	marriage rate
ser/quedarse soltero/a	to be/remain single
la pareja cohabitante/de hecho	unmarried couple
La gente se casa cada vez menos.	People are getting married less and less.
el retraso en la edad del matrimonio	later age of marriage
las parejas sin vínculo matrimonial	couples without marriage ties
la unión consensual	unmarried/consensual union
el matrimonio de los homosexuales, bisexuales y transexuales	homosexual, bisexual and transexual marriage
los nacimientos fuera del matrimonio	births out of wedlock

La boda	***The wedding***
el matrimonio civil	civil wedding
casarse por lo civil	to have a civil wedding
casarse por la iglesia	to have a church wedding
las bodas tradicionales	traditional weddings
la boda informal	informal wedding
el día de la boda	wedding day
el novio	bridegroom
la novia	bride
la dama de honor	bridesmaid
el padrino de boda	best man
el vestido de novia	wedding dress
llevar un velo	to wear a veil

el anillo	ring
los votos matrimoniales	marriage vows
el salón de bodas	wedding venue
el banquete de bodas	wedding banquet/breakfast
la invitación	invitation
los invitados	guests
gastar mucho en una boda	to spend a lot on a wedding
los arreglos florales	flower arrangements
el/la fotógrafo/a	photographer
el grupo musical	musical group
los recién casados	newly weds
la luna de miel	honeymoon

Los altibajos en el matrimonio	***The ups and downs of marriage***
entenderse bien/mal llevarse bien/mal	to get on well/badly
la felicidad	happiness
el respaldo mutuo	mutual support
(in)fiel	(un)faithful
unido/a	united
estable	stable
el respeto	respect
la buena voluntad	good will
el afecto	affection, warmth
el cariño	love, affection
cariñoso/a	affectionate
encariñarse	to grow fond of, to get attached to
la (in)tolerancia	(in)tolerance
la (in)fidelidad	(in)fidelity
extramatrimonial	extramarital
la disputa matrimonial	marital dispute
la crisis matrimonial	marriage crisis
el rompimiento conyugal	marriage breakdown
el adulterio	adultery
el rechazo	rejection
sentir celos	to feel jealous
los malos tratos	ill-treatment, abuse

El divorcio	***Divorce***
estar divorciado/a	to be divorced
el divorcio más frecuente	more frequent divorce
solicitar un divorcio	to apply for a divorce

el divorcio contencioso	contested divorce
la tasa de divorcio	divorce rate
el/la consejero/a de orientación matrimonial	marriage guidance counsellor
el consejo	advice
los trámites de divorcio	divorce procedures
iniciar los procedimientos del divorcio	to initiate divorce proceedings
el alejamiento	estrangement
un proceso penoso	a painful process
la ruptura matrimonial	marriage break-up
ser incompatibles	to be incompatible
cuando un matrimonio se deshace	when a marriage breaks up
la separación	separation
separarse de mutuo acuerdo	to separate by mutual agreement
hijos, bienes y posesiones	children, property and possessions
ejercer la guarda	to have custody
la pensión alimenticia	(spousal) maintenance
culpar	to blame
la culpa	blame
hablar mal	to disparage, to put down
el reparto de bienes	sharing of goods/property
el/la abogado/a	lawyer
el juzgado	court
la conciliación	reconciliation
volver a casarse	to remarry

Websites

https://elpais.com/tag/familia/a

http://enfamilia.aeped.es

www.hacerfamilia.com

www.tiposdefamilias.com

Strategy

The idea of a 'family' of words refers to the existence of groups of words with a common root. Thus, *zapato* (shoe) gives rise to *zapatero/a* (cobbler) and *zapatería* (shoe shop). Be aware that a family of words can also contain words with prefixes, e.g. the root word *rico* (rich) gives rise to *enriquecer* (to enrich).

A Busca palabras de la misma familia y tradúcelas al inglés. Encontrarás algunas palabras en el vocabulario.

1 amor
2 cuidado
3 familia
4 fértil
5 hermano/a
6 jubilación
7 materno/a
8 sexo
9 soltar
10 tolerar

B Sustituye la palabra en cursiva por un sinónimo adecuado.

1 Casi todos mis *familiares* viven en Barcelona.
2 María quiere divorciarse pero su *esposo* no está de acuerdo
3 Mi hijo y otro chico *viven juntos* felizmente en un piso en Zaragoza.
4 No sé por qué la familia de Laura no me invitó *al casamiento*.
5 Todo el mundo *criticaba a* Juan por qué solía maltratar a su mujer.
6 Hoy en día muchos *progenitores* deben conciliar su vida profesional con sus responsabilidades familiares.
7 Pedro y Javier *consiguieron* comprar un piso en el barrio madrileño de Chueca.
8 Emilio *se casó de nuevo* el sábado pasado.

C Escribe el verbo que deriva de los sustantivos siguientes y traduce el verbo al inglés.

	Verbo	**Traducción**
la convivencia		
la acogida		
el cambio		
el aborto		
la separación		
la promesa		
el lazo		
la relación		
la conducta		
el alejamiento		

2 El mundo laboral

La vida laboral en España y las actitudes hacia el trabajo — *Working life in Spain and attitudes to work*

Vocabulario clave	***Key vocabulary***
el comercio	business, commerce, business studies
el/la director(a)	director, manager
el/la empleador(a)	employer
el/la empresario/a	entrepreneur, businessman/woman, employer
la compañía / la empresa	company, firm
cobrar / ganar	to earn
la formación profesional	vocational training
la agencia de colocación	employment agency
el/la empleado/a	employee
el/la trabajador(a) / el/la obrero/a	worker

En general	***In general***
la producción industrial	industrial production
la industrialización	industrialisation
las grandes empresas	major companies
la multinacional	multinational company
el emprendimiento	entrepreneurship
el coste de la mano de obra	labour costs
crear su propia empresa	to start your own business
la economía sumergida	black economy
SEPE (el Servicio Público de Empleo Estatal)	State agency dealing with employment and benefits
Ministerio de Empleo y Seguridad Social	Ministry of Employment and Social Security
jubilarse	to retire

El personal	***Staff, personnel***
el puesto de alta dirección	senior management position
el/la director(a) general	managing director
el/la director(a) de ventas	sales manager

el/la director(a) de personal	personnel manager
los altos cargos	top people
la oficina central	head office
el/la secretario/a de dirección	management secretary
el/la jefe/a	boss
el/la encargado/a	foreman/woman
la plantilla	staff
la mano de obra	workforce
el/la funcionario/a	civil servant
el/la peón/peona	unskilled worker
el peonaje	unskilled workforce, labourers
el/la trabajador(a) eventual	casual worker
el/la jornalero/a	day labourer
un trabajo de cuello blanco	a white-collar job
ser trabajador(a) autónomo/a	to be self-employed
experimentado/a	experienced
generar empleo	to generate employment
cambiar de empleo	to change jobs
el estatus	status

Las condiciones del trabajo	***Working conditions***
el mercado de trabajo	labour market
la rentabilidad	profitability
la productividad	productivity
la competencia	competition
la creación de empleo	creation of employment
el lugar de trabajo	workplace
el contrato	contract
contratar	to contract, to take on
el contrato basura	abusive contract
el sector de servicios	service sector
la banca	banking
la sucursal	branch
la población obrera	working population
el trabajo a tiempo completo	full-time work
el trabajo a tiempo parcial	part-time work
el trabajo a destajo	piece work
el horario de trabajo	working hours
el trabajo con horario flexible	flexitime job
la flexibilización de horarios	flexitime
el trabajo por turnos	shiftwork

trabajar horas extra	to work overtime
el pluriempleo	having more than one job
asalariado/a	waged, salaried
el sueldo	pay, salary
la nómina	payroll, salary
las posibilidades de ascenso	promotion possibilities
las normas de seguridad	safety regulations
la subida de salario el aumento de sueldo	pay rise
el salario/sueldo mínimo	minimum wage
Las relaciones laborales	***Labour relations***
el sindicato	trade union
el sindicalismo	trade unionism
el/la sindicalista	trade unionist
UGT (Unión General de Trabajadores)	General Workers' Union (Spanish trade union)
CC.OO. (Comisiones Obreras)	Workers' Commissions (Spanish trade union)
exigir retribuciones mejores	to demand better remuneration
las vacaciones retribuidas/pagadas	paid holidays
el coste de la mano de obra	labour costs
el derecho a la huelga	right to strike
ponerse en huelga ir a la huelga	to go on strike
la convocatoria	strike call
convocar manifestaciones	to call demonstrations
reivindicar	to claim, to demand
la reivindicación	claim, demand
la huelga salvaje	wildcat strike
las negociaciones	negotiations
negociar	to negotiate
la patronal	management
El paro	***Unemployment***
el desempleo	unemployment
el paro	unemployment, stoppage
el paro a largo plazo	long-term unemployment
las cifras del paro	unemployment figures
la tasa del desempleo	unemployment rate
los costes salariales	wage costs

la prestación el subsidio	benefit
la prestación de paro el subsidio de desempleo	dole
apuntarse al paro	to sign on the dole
cobrar el paro	to claim unemployment benefit
el recorte de personal	downsizing of staff
despedir	to sack, to fire, to dismiss
el despido	redundancy
la compensación por despido	redundancy pay
estar parado/a estar desempleado/a	to be unemployed
los parados los desempleados	the unemployed
reciclar a alguien	to retrain somebody
reciclarse	to retrain (i.e. to get retrained)
el reciclaje	retraining
dimitir	to resign
adaptarse a los cambios	to adapt to changes

Las actitudes hacia el trabajo	***Attitudes to work***
la satisfacción laboral la satisfacción en el trabajo	job satisfaction
los empleados satisfechos	satisfied employees
la mano de obra satisfecha	satisfied workforce
un alto nivel de satisfacción	a high level of satisfaction
un/a trabajador(a) descontento/a	a dissatisfied worker
una actitud de trabajo positiva/negativa	a positive/negative attitude to work
sentirse relajado/a en el entorno de trabajo	to feel relaxed in the working environment
sentirse a gusto en el trabajo	to feel happy in one's work
el comportamiento (in)deseable	(un)desirable behaviour
el comportamiento de grupo	group behaviour
desempeñarse bien/mal	to perform well/badly
un empleado de alto desempeño	a high-performance employeee
la colaboración	collaboration, cooperation
el liderazgo	leadership
la motivación	motivation
el esfuerzo personal	personal commitment
el compromiso con el trabajo bien hecho	commitment to a job well done

la creencia en los valores de la empresa	belief in the values of the company
el compromiso organizacional	commitment to the organisation
identificarse con las metas de la organización	to identify with the goals of the organisation
la evaluación favorable/desfavorable	favourable/unfavourable appraisal
el absentismo	absenteeism
sentirse rechazado/a	to feel rejected
sentir que uno no vale nada	to feel worthless
el/la perezoso/a	idler
un(a) "nini" ("ni trabaja ni estudia")	NEET (not in employment, education or training)

Las oportunidades de trabajo para los jóvenes — *Job opportunities for young people*

Vocabulario clave	***Key vocabulary***
la ambición	ambition
el/la aprendiz(a)	apprentice
el aprendizaje	apprenticeship
tomarse un año libre	to take a gap year/year out
la salida laboral	job opportunity
la experiencia laboral la oportunidad laboral	work experience
las demandas del mercado	market demands

En general	***In general***
la esperanza	hope
tener ganas de (hacer)	to feel like (doing), be eager to (do)
ahorrar	to save (up)
emanciparse	to leave home
empezar su propia vida	to start one's own life
las perspectivas laborales	job prospects
entrar al/en el mundo laboral	to access the job market
trasladar	to relocate
conseguir el primer empleo	to get one's first job
ganarse la vida	to earn a living
aprender	to learn
ser puntual	to be punctual
la empresa familiar	family business

hacer negocio con	to do business with
hacer contactos	to network
el contacto	contact (person)
la vacante	vacancy
cubrir una baja	to cover an absence
instalarse en el extranjero	to establish oneself abroad
el trabajo esporádico	occasional job
la competencia	competence, capability
la competitividad feroz	fierce competition
el sector público	public sector
el sector privado	private sector
el sector servicios	services sector
las Pequeñas y Medianas Empresas (PYMEs)	Small and Medium-sized Enterprises (SMEs)
la hostelería	catering and hotel management
el turismo	tourism
la gestión de mercancías	retail management
las ventas y el marketing	sales and marketing
las tecnologías de la información	information technology

Los contratos laborales	***Work contracts***
el contrato fijo	permanent contract
el contrato a tiempo completo	full-time contract
el contrato temporal	temporary contract
el contrato a tiempo parcial	part-time contract
el contrato de prácticas	internship
el contrato de prueba	probationary contract
el contrato no remunerado	unpaid contract
el contrato precario	insecure contract

La experiencia, la formación y las cualificaciones	***Experience, training and qualifications***
el/la titulado/a universitario/a	person with a university degree
la formación académica	formal/academic education
la titulación académica	academic qualifications
los títulos académicos	academic qualifications
con licenciatura en...	with a degree in...
la experiencia profesional	professional/work experience
la cualificación profesional	professional qualification
la formación profesional dual	sandwich courses (combined course with work and study)

los requisitos	requirements
aprobar	to pass (exams)
la habilidad la destreza	skill
el talento	talent
la capacidad	capacity
capacitado/a	qualified
equiparse	to equip oneself
ajustarse a	to adapt to
familiarizarse	to familiarise oneself
formarse	to train
necesitar experiencia	to need experience
tener experiencia	to have experience
dominar idiomas	to have a good grasp of languages
dominar perfectamente el inglés/el alemán/el francés	to speak fluent English/German/French
hablar italiano con soltura	to speak Italian fluently
tener un año de experiencia en...	to have a year's experience in...
la beca	grant
hacer oposiciones	to seek a job by public competition (mainly in Spanish Civil Service)
el trabajo voluntario	voluntary work

Solicitar trabajo	***Applying for jobs***
el puesto	post
el consejo	advice
un trabajo muy solicitado	a much sought-after job
andar en busca de empleo	to be on the lookout for a job
solicitar un puesto de trabajo	to apply for a job
la solicitud de trabajo	job application
la hoja de solicitud	application form
escribir una carta de solicitud	to write a letter of application
me permito dirigirme a usted para (+ *inf*)	I am writing to you in order to...
el currículum vitæ	curriculum vitæ, CV
mandar el currículum	to send your CV
entregar el CV en mano	to hand over your CV
el anuncio	advertisement
leer en las 'ofertas de trabajo'	to read in the 'Situations Vacant'
responder a un anuncio	to reply to an advert

se necesita fontanero/camarero/ chófer	plumber/waiter/driver required
los datos personales	personal information/data
pedir informes/referencias	to ask for references
dar informes/referencias	to give references, act as referee
las aficiones	interests
ofrecer mis servicios como…	to offer my services as…
la entrevista	interview
entrevistar bien	to interview well
ir bien vestido/a	to be well/smartly dressed
ser apto/a para el trabajo	to be suitable for the job
ofrecer el trabajo	to offer the job
incorporarse al trabajo lo antes posible	to go out to work as soon as possible
conseguir un trabajo por enchufe	to get a job through connections/by pulling strings
estar bien enchufado/a	to have good connections, to be well connected
Me rechazaron.	They turned me down.
el rechazo	rejection, refusal
rechazar el puesto	to turn the job down
los recursos humanos	human resources
Las ambiciones	***Ambitions***
ser ambicioso/a	to be ambitious
tener vocación	to have a vocation
buscarse una carrera en informática	to seek a career in information technology
planificar su futuro	to plan one's future
tomar la iniciativa	to take the initiative
aprovechar la oportunidad	to take the opportunity
hacer un esfuerzo	to make an effort
el esfuerzo personal	personal commitment
apuntar alto	to aim high
poner las miras en un puesto alto	to set one's sights on a top job
llegar a la cima de su profesión	to reach the top of one's professsion
independizarse	to become independent
mantenerse informado/a	to keep oneself informed
comunicarse bien	to communicate well
sacar adelante la carrera	to advance one's career
aspirar a periodista	to have aspirations to be a journalist
prepararse para fontanero/a	to train as a plumber

seguir un curso de ingeniería	to follow a course in engineering
hacer un aprendizaje en carpintería	to do a carpentry apprenticeship
estudiar para abogado/a	to study to become a lawyer
trabajar de camarero/a a la espera de una mejor oportunidad laboral	to work as a waiter while waiting for a better job opportunity
ahorrar para el futuro	to save up the future
promocionar la imagen	to promote one's image
el potencial adquisitivo	earnings potential
tener su propia empresa	to run one's own business
el/la autónomo/a	self-employed person
competir	to compete

La igualdad de género — *Gender equality*

Vocabulario clave	***Key vocabulary***
el mundo laboral	world of work
la desigualdad	inequality
la igualdad de oportunidad	equality of opportunity
la incorporación de la mujer en el trabajo	involvement/acceptance of women in the workplace
la carrera profesional	professional career
equitativo/a	fair, equitable
el género	gender
la discriminación de género	gender discrimination
el prejuicio	prejudice
el acoso sexual	sexual harassment
luchar	to fight, to struggle

En general	***In general***
la actividad laboral	work activity
el oficio	job, trade
la tarea	task
la oferta de mano de obra	labour supply
el salario por hora	hourly rate of pay
el sueldo promedio	average salary
erradicar	to eradicate
la desventaja	disadvantage
la soltera	single woman
el sexo femenino/masculino	female/male sex

El empleo actual de las mujeres	***Present-day employment of women***
el derecho a trabajar	right to work
incorporarse al mercado laboral	to enter the job market
el ingreso en el mercado laboral	entry to the job market
adaptarse a las necesidades del mercado	to adapt to the needs of the market
la inserción de las mujeres	inclusion of women
desempeñar un puesto	to hold a post
la mujer asalariada	salaried woman
la oportunidad	opportunity
la creciente participación de las mujeres casadas	increasing participation of married women
poder diversificar su elección	to be able to widen one's choice
la discriminación positiva	positive discrimination
empoderarse	to empower oneself
el eslogan	slogan
igual salario por igual trabajo	equal pay for equal work
merecer	to deserve
el valor	value
ascender	to be promoted
el éxito	success
lograr	to succeed
la libertad	freedom
la liberación	liberation, freeing
romper estereotipos	to break down stereotypes
una relación de igualdad entre hombres y mujeres	an equal relationship between men and women
la igualdad con los hombres en su nivel de ingresos	equality with men in their income level
garantizar la paridad de género	to guarantee gender parity
la igualdad entre hombres y mujeres	equality between men and women
reivindicar derechos como trabajadoras	to demand rights as female workers
las medidas para evitar la discriminación	measures to avoid discrimination
la legislación a favor de la mujer	legislation in favour of women
Ley de Igualdad (España, 2007)	Equal Opportunities Act (Spain, 2007)
el juicio	judgement
los derechos humanos	human rights
mejorar	to improve
la toma de conciencia	awareness raising

la formación educativa	educational training
el mayor acceso a la formación	better access to training
el desarrollo profesional	professional development
la jornada completa	full workday
la jornada laboral	working day
la jornada reducida	shorter working day
tener libertad de horario	to have flexitime
el incremento del trabajo autónomo	increase in self-employment
el horario flexible	flexible hours
trabajar desde casa	to work from home
la tasa de actividad laboral femenina	the rate of female employment
la tasa de desempleo femenino	the rate of female unemployment
la reducción de la tasa de natalidad	reduction in the birth rate
la ejecutiva	businesswoman
la directora ejecutiva	(female) executive director

El impacto en la vida doméstica	***The impact on family life***
sacar adelante a la familia	to provide for the family
buscar el equilibrio entre el trabajo y la vida personal	to seek a work–life balance
conciliar la vida familiar y profesional	to reconcile work and family life
tener que sacar adelante el trabajo de fuera y dentro de la casa	to have to do work outside and inside the home
la trabajadora con cargas familiares	female worker with family responsibilities
seguir realizando las tareas domésticas	to continue to carry out housework
el ama (*f*) de casa	housewife
el cuidado del hogar	household care
tener una doble jornada de trabajo	to have a double working day/workload
cansarse	to get tired
los quehaceres domésticos	household chores
compartir las tareas domésticas	to share the housework
ayudar en casa	to help out with household chores
cuidar de los hijos	to take care of the children
compartir responsabilidades	to share responsibilities
solicitar un permiso para el cuidado de los hijos	to ask for leave to look after the children
el permiso de maternidad/paternidad	maternity/paternity leave

la excedencia por cuidado de los niños	parental leave
cogerse una excedencia	to arrange unpaid leave
la planificación familiar	family planning
quedarse embarazada	to get pregnant
la baja por maternidad	maternity leave
la guardería	crèche
el período de inactividad	period out of work/inactivity
volver al mundo laboral	to return to the world of work
el impacto de la ausencia de los padres sobre los niños	the impact of parental absence on the children
dedicar tiempo a la familia	to devote time to the family
El padre que trabaja largas jornadas dedica poco tiempo a los hijos.	The father who works long hours devotes little time to his children.
compartir la crianza de los hijos	to share the upbringing of the children
la falta de tiempo de los padres con los hijos	lack of time spent by parents with their children

La discriminación en el trabajo	***Discrimination at work***
una cuestión de actitudes	a question of attitudes
desfavorecido/a	disadvantaged, underprivileged
discriminatorio/a	discriminatory
la discriminación salarial	wage discrimination
la discriminación por razón de sexo	sexual/gender discrimination
las desigualdades entre varones y mujeres	inequality between men and women
la desigualdad entre los sexos	inequality between the sexes
la desigualdad persistente	persistent inequality
el estereotipo	stereotype
los estereotipos sexuales	gender stereotypyes
cobrar el [x]% por ciento menos	to earn [x]% per cent less
estar peor pagadas que los hombres	to be less well paid than men
el techo de cristal	glass ceiling
pocas ocupan los altos cargos	few occupy the top jobs
protestar por los bajos sueldos	to protest at low salaries
la brecha salarial	wages gap
sentirse frustrado/a	to feel frustrated
desencantado/a	disillusioned
desmoralizarse	to become disheartened
ser luchador(a)	to be a fighter

controvertido/a	controversial
la polémica	controversy
el respeto	respect
aguantar	to endure, to put up with
la víctima	victim
el machismo	male chauvinism
la discriminación por sexo	sexism
las conductas masculinas	male behaviour
acosar	to harass
la vejación	harassment, humiliation
el abuso de poder	abuse of power
el depredador sexual	sexual predator
privar	to deprive
despreciar	to scorn
infravalorar	to undervalue
la desvalorización de la mujer	devaluing of women
el patriarcado	patriarchy
patriarcal	patriarchal
mandar	to order, to be in command
mandón/mandona	bossy, domineering
dominar	to dominate
la dominación	domination
dominante	dominant
ejercer control y autoridad	to exercise control and authority
la falta de respeto	lack of respect
el privilegio	privilege
rechazar	to reject
inferior	inferior
superior	superior
varonil	male, manly

Websites

www.sepe.es

www.ugt.es

www.ccoo.es

Strategy

Many word in Spanish have more than one meaning. They may be linked semantically, e.g. *el paro* means 'unemployment' and 'stoppage'; they can also have competely different meanings, e.g. *banco*-'bank' and 'bench'.

A Mira las siguientes palabras, luego traduce las frases que siguen al inglés. ¡Las palabras tienen al menos dos significados!

1 despedir
Ayer la empresa *despidió* a 100 empleados.
Isabel estaba llorando cuando nos *despedimos* de ella.

2 modelo
Mi prima tenía mucho éxito como *modelo* de alta costura.
Antes de construir el polideportivo hicieron un *modelo* a escala.

3 oposición
Si quieres trabajar como profesor en España tienes que preparar *oposiciones*.
En el parlamento la *oposición* cumple una importante función democrática.

4 título
Las universidades dan un *título* académico a los estudiantes que han completado satisfactoriamente su curso.
¿Cuáles el *título* de la nueva novela de Vargas Llosa?

5 carrera
¿Qué *carrera* universitaria vas a realizar?
Hay varios tipos de *carreras* en las pistas de atletismo.

6 cargos
Los *cargos* de terrorismo contra los dos hombres eran falsos.
Los altos *cargos* de la empresa van a reunirse mañana.

B Escribe un adjetivo que deriva de los sustantivos siguientes y traduce el adjetivo al inglés.

	Adjetivo	**Traducción**
la actividad		
la agresión		
la ambición		
la autonomía		
la desigualdad		
el embarazo		
el hogar		
la igualdad		

3 El impacto turístico en España

El impacto económico — *The impact on the economy*

Vocabulario clave	***Key vocabulary***
el/la turista	tourist
el/la visitante	visitor
la inversión	investment
los ingresos	income, earnings
los beneficios	benefits, gains
el presupuesto	budget
rentable	profitable
el desarrollo	development
el PIB (Producto Interior Bruto)	GDP (Gross Domestic Product)
estimular	to encourage, to stimulate
la temporada	season

La economía	***The economy***
la oferta turística	tourist offer/services
la relación precio–calidad	price–quality ratio
el coste del alojamiento	cost of accommodation
el gasto medio diario	average daily expenditure
el gasto medio por turista	average expenditure per tourist
el poder adquisitivo	purchasing power
los turistas con gran capacidad de gasto	tourists with a lot of spending power
una de las principales fuentes de divisas	one of the principal sources of foreign exchange
invertir	to invest
representar el [x]% del PIB español	to represent [x] % of the Spanish GDP
un aumento del PIB del sector turístico	an increase in the GDP of the tourist sector
el empleo	employment, job
el empleo turístico	employment in tourism
El turismo proporciona trabajo a 2,5 millones de personas.	Tourism provides work for 2.5 million people.
la importancia del turismo en el mercado laboral	importance of tourism in the job market

el peso del turismo	importance of tourism
el turismo, motor de la economía	tourism, the driving force of the economy
la rentabilidad	profitability
la mayor rentabilidad	greater profitability
rentabilizar mejor las infraestructuras	to make the infrastructure more profitable
las rebajas de precio	price reductions
un impulso para el crecimiento	a boost for growth
el ritmo de crecimiento	rate of growth
un elevado crecimiento potencial	a high growth potential
España ocupa la tercera posición en el ranking mundial del turismo.	Spain is third in the world tourism rankings.
los datos	data
la cifra	figure, number
la estadística	statistics
desarrollar el interior	to develop inland areas
construir autopistas	to build motorways
aumentar la capacidad de los aeropuertos	to increase airport capacity

Los visitantes	***Visitors***
el/la visitante extranjero/a	foreign visitor
el flujo de visitantes	visitor flow
75 millones de llegadas de visitantes extranjeros	75 million arrivals of foreign visitors
España está a tope de turistas.	Spain is bursting with tourists.
un récord histórico de llegadas	a historic record of arrivals
las previsiones para este año	forecasts for this year
la estancia	stay
alargar las estancias	to extend stays
la ocupación en los meses veraniegos/invernales	occupancy in the summer/winter months
la estacionalidad	seasonal variation (of demand)
el patrón estacional	seasonal pattern
la temporada alta/baja	high/low season
las épocas de alta/baja demanda	times of high/low demand
a mediados de	mid- (week, month etc.)
las pernoctaciones	overnight stays
pernoctar	to stay overnight
la plaza hotelera	hotel bed/vacancy
viajar en una línea de bajo coste	to travel with a low-cost carrier

el número de pasajeros	number of passengers
la capacidad de cada aeropuerto	capacity of each airport
el/la pasajero/a de la clase turista	tourist class passenger
la ruta turística	tourist route

La industria turística	***The tourist industry***
las empresas de turismo	tourist companies
la oficina de turismo	tourist office
el patronato de turismo	tourist board
el centro acreditado	officially recognised centre
España es un país turísticamente muy organizado.	Spain is a well-organised tourist country.
un destino turístico líder	a leading tourist destination
desarrollar la actividad	to develop/carry out activity
la evolución de la actividad turística	development of tourist activity
el alojamiento	accommodation
la restauración	restaurant industry
el sector de la hostelería	hotel and catering sector
los motores de la recuperación	engines of recovery
la mejoría del turismo	improvement in tourism
recuperar terreno	to recover lost ground
promover el turismo rural	to promote rural tourism
el/la constructor(a)	builder
el/la promotor(a) inmobiliario	property developer
el/la especulador(a)	speculator
los profesionales del turismo	tourist professionals
el alquiler	hire
el vehículo de alquiler	rental car
el alquiler de autos	car hire
el vuelo	flight
el folleto	brochure
las recomendaciones	recommendations

Las oportunidades que ofrece el turismo / *The opportunities offered by tourism*

Vocabulario clave	***Key vocabulary***
el/la touroperador(a)	tour operator
el/la agente de viajes	travel agent
el destino	destination
el paquete	package

la industria hotelera	hotel industry
la calidad	quality
el/la cliente	client, customer
gastar	to spend
las tendencias	trends
el clima	climate
el estilo de vida	way of life

Los puestos de trabajo en turismo	***Jobs in tourism***
la formación profesional en turismo	professional training in tourism
las salidas profesionales en turismo	job opportunities in tourism
el chef de cocina	head chef
el/la intérprete	interpreter
el/la encargado/a de seguridad	safety officer
el/la gerente de restaurante	restaurant manager
el/la gerente de hotel	hotel manager
los talleres de habilidades	skills workshops
beneficiarse de	to benefit from
aprovechar	to take advantage of
mejorar	to improve
cobrar	to earn
la calificación de cinco estrellas	five-star rating
la calidad de los servicios	the quality of services
la asequibilidad	affordability, accessibility
la guía de viajes	travel guide
el/la guía turístico/a	tourist guide (person)
los viajes con guía	guided tours
los viajes organizados	organised trips
el servicio al cliente	customer service
la imagen de marca	brand image
en el campo del turismo en el ámbito del turismo	in the field of tourism
estar en auge	to be on the up/booming

Tourism activities	***Las actividades turísticas***
visitar monumentos y museos	to visit monuments and museums
disfrutar de la experiencia	to enjoy the experience
la ciudad monumental	historic town
la zona monumental	historic area
el casco antiguo	old part (of town)
la zona costera	coastal area

los tipos de ocio	types of leisure
las vacaciones de aventura	adventure holidays
el parque temático	theme park
el crucero	cruise; cruise liner
el senderismo	hiking
la estación de esquí	ski resort
el alpinismo	mountain climbing
para todos los gustos	for all tastes
el viajero rural	rural traveller
el turismo interno	domestic tourism
el puente (de mayo)	long weekend (e.g. May)

Las oportunidades comerciales	***Business opportunities***
el reto	challenge
el riesgo	risk
el éxito	success
la creación de empresas innovadoras	creation of innovative companies
competir por atraer turistas	to compete to attract tourists
en busca de experiencias diferentes	in search of different experiences
viajar al extranjero por motivos de ocio	to go abroad for (the purpose of) leisure
un destino para hacer compras	a place to go shopping
atraer viajeros interesados en escapadas	to attract tourists interested in short breaks
impulsar más el sector turístico	to promote the tourist sector more
ofrecer paquetes de ocio	to offer leisure packages
realizar promociones	to carry out promotions
ofrecer mucha variedad	to offer a wide variety
la calidad de las tiendas	the quality of the shopping
ofrecer una experiencia de mayor calidad	to offer a higher quality experience
fomentar el turismo de la tercera edad	to stimulate tourism for senior citizens
la creación de empresas en el ámbito del turismo	the creation of companies in the field of tourism
una oferta de paquetes turísticos	an offer of tourism packages
el viaje con todo incluido	package tour
los tratamientos de salud	health treatment
los temas innovadores	innovative themes
los nuevos mercados	new markets
las nuevas formas de viajar	new ways of travelling
ofrecer una experiencia auténtica	to offer an authentic experience

las marcas de lujo	luxury brands
La opción rural sigue creciendo.	The rural option continues to grow.
el aumento de turistas internacionales	increase in international travellers
una demanda que crece rápidamente	a rapidly growing demand
llenar un hotel	to fill a hotel
prometedor(a)	hopeful, promising
la iniciativa	initiative

El alojamiento	***Accommodation***
acogedor(a)	welcoming
el establecimiento	establishment
el apartamento (de vacaciones)	holiday flat
la casa de alquiler	rented property
la segunda vivienda	holiday home
los alojamientos rurales	rural accommodation
la casa de huéspedes	guest house
la cadena de hoteles	hotel chain
el hotel cinco estrellas	five-star hotel
el hotel de lujo	luxury hotel
el parador	high-class state-run hotel
la urbanización turística	tourism development
el albergue juvenil/de juventud	youth hostel
una habitación con vistas al mar	a room with a sea view
la familia anfitrión	host family
los precios asequibles	affordable prices

Los tipos de turismo	***Types of tourism***
el turismo de alpargata	tourism on the cheap
el turismo alternativo	alternative tourism
el turismo blanco	winter (snow sports) tourism
el turismo de aventura	adventure tourism
el turismo de calidad	quality tourism
el turismo de ciudades	city tourism
el turismo cultural	cultural tourism
el turismo de juerga	binge tourism
el turismo de masas	mass tourism
el turismo gastronomíco	food tourism
el turismo náutico	nautical tourism
el turismo rural	rural tourism
el turismo de sol y playa	sun and beach tourism
el turismo sanitario	health tourism

El impacto socioambiental | *The impact on society and the environment*

Vocabulario clave	***Key vocabulary***
el medio ambiente el entorno	environment
el ecoturismo	ecotourism
el turismo sostenible	sustainable tourism
el turismo ecológico el turismo verde	ecological tourism
la naturaleza	nature
el litoral	coast

El aumento del turismo	***The increase in tourism***
la rapidez del desarrollo turístico	speed of the development of tourism
el crecimiento turístico	growth in tourism
los hoteles en primera línea de playa	hotels on the sea-front
descontrolado/a	out of control
polémico/a	controversial
protestar	to protest
la demolición	demolition
vulnerar	to infringe (a law)
las actividades veraniegas	summer activities
el turismo de cruceros	cruise tourism
las aerolíneas	airlines
el combustible	fuel
las atracciones turísticas como:	tourist attractions such as:
los campos de golf	golf courses
las zonas de acampada	camping areas
los cruceros	cruises
los complejos deportivos	sports complexes
las actividades recreacionales	recreational activities
los hoteles de lujo	luxury hotels
los parques nacionales	national parks
las áreas para preservar la vida silvestre	areas to conserve wildlife
las degustaciones de vino	wine tasting
la movida nocturna	night life

El impacto positivo	***Positive impact***
el fuerte desarrollo del sector terciario	strong development of the tertiary sector
la demanda de mano de obra estacional	demand for seasonal labour
crear empleos	to create work
la mejora en las carreteras españolas	improvement in Spanish roads
la conservación de los recursos culturales	preservation of cultural resources
la conservación de la vida silvestre	conservation of wildlife
un impacto benéfico sobre la región	a beneficial impact on the region
un centro turístico de primera categoría	a first-class tourist centre
disfrutar de los productos de la zona	to enjoy local produce
la venta de alimentos típicos de la región	sale of typical regional foods
el crecimiento en la demanda del turismo ecológico	growth in demand for ecological tourism
la concienciación ecológica la concienciación ambiental	environmental awareness
el desarrollo sostenible	sustainable development
la diversidad de las especies	the diversity of species
La biodiversidad fomenta el turismo.	Biodiversity encourages tourism.
el desarrollo de los atractivos culturales	development of cultural attractions
la recogida de desperdicios	waste collection
el reciclaje de materiales de desecho	recycling of waste materials

El impacto negativo	***Negative impact***
las consecuencias no deseadas	undesirable consequences
los efectos adversos	adverse effects
las consecuencias a largo plazo	long-term consequences
nocivo/a dañino/a perjudicial	harmful
la porquería	rubbish, mess
los problemas de masificación	problems of overcrowding
Las playas están a rebosar.	The beaches are overflowing.
el gamberrismo	loutishness, yobbishness
las invasiones de gamberros extranjeros	invasion of foreign yobs

la concentración del turismo en el litoral y los archipiélagos	concentration of tourism on the coast and the islands
el deterioro en las zonas costeras	deterioration of coastal areas
La llegada masiva de turistas conduce:	The massive influx of tourists leads to:
a la mayor cantidad de basura.	greater amount of rubbish.
a más emisiones de gases contaminantes.	more emissions of polluting gases.
al abuso de los recursos naturales.	abuse of natural resources.
al deterioro de los ecosistemas.	the deterioration of eco-systems.
a la degradación del litoral.	degradation of the coast.
al agotamiento de los recursos	the exhausting of resources.
la naturaleza ambiental de la zona receptora	the natural environment of the receiving area
los cambios en el entorno natural	changes in the natural environment
el impacto negativo en el medio ambiente	negative impact on the environment
el impacto de los cruceros en un destino	impact of cruises on a destination
la huella de carbono de la industria turística	carbon footprint of the tourist industry
el uso intensivo de los recursos naturales	intensive use of natural resources
la contaminación del agua/del aire/del suelo	water/air/soil pollution
las emisiones del transporte	transport emissions
las descargas de residuos	discharge of waste
arrojar al mar los residuos	to dump waste into the sea
los gastos de la limpieza de ríos y playas	expenditure on cleaning up rivers and beaches
convertir las fiestas locales en espectáculos para turistas	to turn local festivals into tourist spectacles
amenazar al estilo de vida local	to threaten the local way of life
la brecha cultural entre residentes y visitantes	cultural gap between residents and visitors

Websites

www.spain.info/es

www.esmadrid.com

www.andalucia.org

www.turismoencatalunya.es

A Escribe en inglés el significado correcto de las siguientes palabras con relación al turismo

1 la comodidad
2 la inversión
3 la estación
4 los datos
5 la dirección
6 la renta
7 la parcela
8 la plaza
9 la restauración

B Busca un sinónimo y un antónimo para las palabras siguientes.

	Sinónimo	**Antónimo**
ahorrar		
el adelanto		
ampliar		
comprar		
eliminar		
rápido/a		

Strategy

Many verbs change their meaning when a prefix such as *de(s)* or *re* is added. The new verb often has the opposite meaning, e.g. *crecer* (to increase)/ *decrecer* (to decrease).

C Añade un prefijo a las siguientes palabras para cambiar su sentido. Escribe la traducción de cada palabra en inglés.

	Traducción	**Palabra con prefijo**	**Traducción**
mover			
gastar			
crear			
construir			
controlado/a			
gustar			
coger			
arrollar			
la unión			
el empleo			

Theme 2 Political and artistic culture in the Spanish-speaking world

4 La música

Los cambios y las tendencias — *Changes and trends*

Vocabulario clave	***Key vocabulary***
la industria musical	music industry
el desarrollo	development
la evolución	evolution
la tendencia	trend
la innovación	innovation
innovador(a)	innovative
los archivos de música los ficheros de música	music files
descargar música	to download music
lanzar un sencillo	to release a single
el álbum	album
el sencillo	single
los festivales de música	music festivals
el género	genre (of music)

La evolución de la industria musical	***The evolution of the music industry***
la evolución constante	constant evolution
desarrollar	to develop
la diversidad	diversity
un nuevo desafío	a new challenge
la búsqueda de nuevos sonidos	search for new sounds
los nuevos dispositivos	new devices
la revolución	revolution
revolucionar el gusto del público	to revolutionise public taste
transformar	to transform
reinventarse	to reinvent one/itself
abrirse camino/paso	to break into, to make your way
triunfar	to succeed

La música es cada vez más comercial.	Music is more and more commercial.
el fácil acceso a los productos musicales	easy access to musical products
asociar al artista a una marca	to associate an artist with a brand
un icono global	a global icon
el auge del streaming	rise of streaming
la innovación en música digital	innovation in digital music
las plataformas líderes de música	leading music (software) platforms
la disponibilidad de música gratuita	availability of free music
la industria discográfica	recording/music industry
la discográfica el sello discográfico	record label
los sellos de carácter independiente	independent labels
la revitalización de la música grabada	revival of recorded music
el lanzamiento de un sencillo	release of a single
la herencia musical	musical heritage
la emergencia de nuevos artistas discográficas	emergence of new recording artists
sacar una canción	to bring out a song
promocionar una canción nueva	to promote a new song
fomentar	to promote
lanzar un álbum	to release an album
el estreno de un álbum	release of an album
transmitir en directo	to broadcast live
un premio discográfico otorgado a un artista	a recording prize awarded to an artist
el mercado musical	music market
la banda de música independiente	independent band
el pinchadiscos	disc-jockey, DJ
difundir	to broadcast, to disseminate
la entrevista	interview
la farándula	show business
los medios de comunicación	media
el conservatorio	conservatoire

La reacción del público a la música	***The reaction of the public to music***
la música como estilo de vida/fuerza espiritual/medio de expresión	music as a way of life/a spiritual force/a means of expression
la canción más vendida del año	best-selling song of the year
el mejor álbum del año	best album of the year
ponerse de moda	to be fashionable
pasar de moda	to go out of fashion

la experiencia festival	festival experience
las listas de éxitos	charts
el/la melómano/a	music-lover

Estilos, sonido y ritmo	***Styles, sound and rhythm***
la banda de música	brass band
la música folk/reggae/indie/rock/metal/punk	folk/reggae/indie/rock/metal/punk music
la música alternativa/andina/antigua/clásica/de cámara/étnica/sacra	alternative/Andean/early/classical/chamber/ethnic/sacred
los ritmos urbanos/latinos/caribeños/africanos/salseros	urban/Latin/Caribbean/African/salsa rhythms
fusionarse con ritmos electrónicos	to fuse with electronic rhythms
fusionarse	to blend, to merge
la mezcla de música clásica y flamenco	mixture of classical music and flamenco
experimentar con diferentes estilos musicales	to experiment with different styles of music
la fusión de estilos	fusion of styles
la influencia caribeña	Caribbean influence
la influencia africana/árabe	African/Arab influence
el sonido	sound
rítmico/a	rhythmic
el compás	beat, rhythm
la armonía	harmony
la melodía	melody

Escuchar música	***Listening to music***
la grabación	recording
el disco número uno	number one hit
el álbum de estudio	studio album
el vídeo musical	music video
la pista	track
el/la oyente	listener
los auriculares	headphones
ser aficionado/a a	to be a fan of
seguir una banda	to follow a band
identificarse con un grupo	to identify with a group
la su(b)scripción	subscription
suscribirse a un sitio online de música	to subscribe to a website for online music
la tienda de música en línea	online music store
descargar canciones desde una tienda de música	to download songs from a music store

escuchar música en el móvil (*Sp*)/celular (*LAm*)	to listen to music on the mobile
escuchar música con un reproductor de MP3	to listen to music with an MP3 player
transmitir los archivos de música	to stream music files
escuchar música sin pagar	to listen to music without paying for it
infringir la ley	to break the law
la música pirateada	pirated music
las descargas ilegales	illegal downloads
descargar música (i)legalmente	to download music (il)legally

El impacto de la música en la cultura contemporánea

The impact of music on contemporary culture

Vocabulario clave	***Key vocabulary***
el/la músico/a	musician
el/la cantante	singer
cantar	to sing
la canción	song
la letra	lyrics, words (of a song)
el concierto	gig, concert
la estrella de pop	pop star
la música pop	pop music
el baile / la danza	dance
componer	to compose
la composición	composition
el/la compositor(a)	composer
el coro	choir
tocar	to play (a musical instrument)
la interpretación / la actuación	performance
la obra	work (musical)
el ritmo	rhythm
la influencia	influence
influyente	influential

Los modelos a seguir	***Role models***
el/la artista predilecta	favourite artist
el ídolo de pop	pop idol

la carrera	career
el éxito	success
el talento	talent
la fama	fame
llegar a la cima	to reach the top
sin igual	unrivalled
el icono	icon
carismático/a	charismatic
impactante	striking, impressive
el magnetismo	magnetism, charisma
prestigioso/a	prestigious
dedicarse a	to devote oneself to
la pasión	passion
apasionado/a	passionate
increíble	incredible
legendario/a	legendary
expresivo/a	expressive
la superestrella	superstar
el culto al héroe	hero-worship
el vestuario	(artist's) wardrobe, clothes
la vestimenta	clothing, outfit
el atractivo físico	physical attraction
controvertido/a	controversial
admirar	to admire
adorar	to adore
chiflar (*coll*)	to like
identificarse con	to identify (oneself) with
idealizar	to idealise
idolatrar	to idolise
venerar	to worship
seguir los ídolos musicales	to follow music idols
impresionar	to impress
influenciar en influir en	to have an influence on
influenciado/a por	influenced by
ejercer influencia en	to exert influence on
dar ejemplo	to set an example
inspirar	to inspire

---

imitar el comportamiento de un ídolo	to copy the behaviour of an idol
imitar a su artista predilecta	to imitate one's favourite artist
imitar la forma de vestirse	to imitate the style of dress

imitar la forma de hablar	to imitate the way of speaking
buscar la identidad	to search for identity
influenciado/a por las letras de sus canciones preferidas	influenced by the lyrics of one's favourite songs
implantar valores	to establish/implant values
determinar el comportamiento juvenil	to determine young people's behaviour
una mala influencia sobre los jóvenes	a bad influence on the young
el uso de las drogas	use of drugs
tomar drogas	to take drugs
la mala conducta	bad behaviour
el impacto del vestuario de los artistas	impact of clothes worn by artists
el enorme impacto del reggae	huge impact of reggae

Los cantantes	***Singers***
el/la rockero/a	rock singer
los pioneros de la música rock	pioneers of rock music
el/la artista	artist
el rapero	rapper
el conjunto pop el grupo de pop	pop group
la agrupación musical	music group/ensemble
el/la músico/a ambulante	busker
tocar música en la calle	to busk

La actuación	***Performance***
el evento musical	musical event
poner un programa	to put on a show
la sala de conciertos	concert hall
la sala de fiestas	night club
el auditorio	concert hall, auditorium
ir a ver una banda en vivo	to go to see a live band
la música en directo la música en vivo	live music
el concierto por la paz	peace concert
el concierto en vivo	live concert
disfrutar de música en directo	to enjoy live music
ver a sus artistas favoritas en vivo	to see one's favorite artists live
ir de gira	to go on a tour
una gira internacional	an international tour
el estreno	first appearance; premiere
el festival pop	pop festival
actuar	to act, to perform
el/la director(a)	conductor

interpretar	to perform
la voz	voice
el/la intérprete	performer
el escenario	stage, setting
la escena	stage, scene
entrar en escena	to go on stage
el espectáculo	show, spectacle
la audiencia el público	audience, public
los fans	fans
el/la espectador(a)	spectator
emitir	to broadcast
el altavoz	speaker
amplificar	to amplify
el micrófono	microphone
los focos	lights
el sistema de amplificación	PA system
los amplificadores	loudspeakers, amplifiers
el teclado	keyboard
tocar la batería	to play drums
tocar la guitarra eléctrica	to play electric guitar
la improvisación	improvisation
el acompañamiento	accompaniment
el/la telonero/a	opening performer/act
aplaudir	to applaud
apreciar	to appreciate
abuchear	to boo
emocionarse	to get excited
vocear	to shout, to scream, to cheer
inolvidable	unforgettable

Instrumentos e instrumentalistas	***Instruments and instrumentalists***
el/la instrumentalista	instrumentalist
el instrumento de metal/de percusión/ de viento/cuerda	brass/percussion/wind/string instrument
tocar un instrumento	to play an instrument
tocar la flauta	to play the flute
el/la guitarrista	guitarist
el piano	piano
el/la pianista	pianist
el tambor	drum
la trompeta	trumpet
el/la solista	soloist

La diversidad de la música hispana	***The diversity of Hispanic music***
la música contemporána/clásica/coral/religiosa/folklórica/amerindia/andina/caribeña	contemporary/classical/choral/religious/folk/Amerindian/Andean/Caribbean music
heredar	to inherit
la herencia	inheritance
la identidad	identity
la música de la selva peruana	music from the Peruvian jungle
la música de origen indígena	music of native origin
los estilos de origen afroamericano	styles of Afro-American origin
la cultura tanguera	tango culture
las raíces africanas de la rumba	African roots of the rumba
la canción de protesta	protest song
la zarzuela	*zarzuela* (Spanish light opera)

La música y danza	***Music and dance***
el/la bailarín/bailarina el/la danzante	dancer
bailar danzar	to dance
el paso	step
el/la bailaor(a)	dancer (flamenco)
el/la cantaor(a)	flamenco singer (only)
el/la cantautor(a)	singer-songwriter
el cante flamenco	flamenco song
la castañuela	castanets
la pandereta	tambourine
el salón de baile	dance hall
el tablao flamenco	flamenco show
el cante jondo	'deep' song (of flamenco music)
el traje de corto	(man's) flamenco costume
el traje de flamenco	(woman's) flamenco costume
la jota	*jota* (Aragonese dance)
el paso doble	*pasodoble*
la sardana	*sardana* (Catalan dance)

Websites

www.movistarplus.es/cero/pop
https://elpais.com/tag/musica/a
https://elpais.com/tag/danza/a
http://musicandote.com/generos-musicales

A ¿Cuál es el género de las siguientes palabras: masculino, femenino o los dos?

	Masculino	Femenino	Masculino/ Femenino
álbum			
ley			
pasión			
certamen			
festival			
intérprete			
compás			
solista			
auge			
galardón			
voz			
pianista			
oyente			
flauta			
sistema			
identidad			

B Escribe en español un sinónimo para las palabras siguientes.

1 la fama
2 interpretar
3 la audiencia
4 venerar
5 genial
6 controvertido/a
7 divertido/a
8 predilecto/a
9 el archivo
10 el concurso

Strategy

Many Spanish verbs change their meaning when they add a reflexive pronoun and become pronominal verbs, e.g *dormir* (to sleep), *dormirse* (to go to sleep).

C Traduce al inglés los pares de verbos siguientes.

1 acabar/acabarse
2 acostar /acostarse
3 caer/caerse
4 despedir/despedirse
5 divertir/divertirse
6 gastar/gastarse
7 marchar/marcharse
8 mudar/mudarse

5 Los medios de comunicación

La televisión y las telenovelas — *Television and soap operas*

Vocabulario clave	***Key vocabulary***
la televisión	television (medium)
la tele	telly
el televisor	television (set)
el/la televidente el/la telespectador(a)	viewer (of televisión)
el programa	programme
el canal la cadena	channel
la telenovela el culebrón	soap opera
la audiencia el público	audience

En general	***In general***
durar	to last
dirigir	to direct
el/la directora(a)	director
el talento	talent
el éxito rotundo	roaring success
el exitazo	great success
la imagen (*pl* imágenes)	image
el título	title
el índice de audiencia	audience ratings
ser aficionado/a a	to be keen on
poner un programa	to put on a programme
tratar un tema	to tackle a theme
ver la televisión	to watch television
hacer zapping	to change channels, to zap
la telebasura	trashy TV

El sistema y los aparatos	***The system and equipment***
poner/quitar la tele	to turn the telly on/off
encender	to switch on
apagar	to switch off

el aparato el receptor	set, receiver
la programación	programme times
una gama amplia de canales	a wide range of channels
la pantalla chica la pequeña pantalla	the small screen
la 'caja tonta'	TV, box (*slang*)
el mando a distancia el control remoto (*LAm*)	remote control
la televisión por cable	cable television
la televisión por satélite	satellite television
el interruptor	switch
el volumen	volume
la antena	aerial
la emisión la retransmisión	broadcast
transmitir emitir	to broadcast
transmitir en directo transmitir en vivo	to broadcast live
la emisión en diferido	recorded programme
grabar	to record
la grabación	recording
la cámara	camera
la pantalla	screen
el plató	television set (e.g. in studio)

El contenido	***Programme content***
el/la locutor(a)	announcer, newcaster
el/la presentador(a)	host, television presenter
presentar	to present, to host
el actor	actor
la actriz	actor/actress
el maquillaje	make-up
el vestuario	wardrobe
el personaje	character
la personalidad	personality
el/la concursante	competitor
el/la artista	artist
desempeñar un papel	to play a part

el papel principal	leading role
interpretar	to interpret; to perform
el/la intérprete	performer
la interpretación	performance
anunciar	to announce
las noticias	news
salir por la tele	to appear on television
entrevistar	to interview
adaptar	to adapt
la adaptación	adaptation
el guión	script
el escenario	scene, setting
el reportaje	report
el subtítulo	subtitle
la crítica	review, criticism
el anuncio	advertisement
la publicidad	advertising, publicity
publicitario/a	advertising
el corte comercial	commercial break
la violencia televisiva	television violence
el vídeo	video (all senses)
el DVD (*dé-uve-dé*)	DVD
grabar en DVD	to record on DVD
entretener(se)	to entertain (oneself), to amuse (oneself)
entretenido/a divertido/a	amusing, entertaining
el entretenimiento la diversión	entertainment, amusement
relajante	relaxing
informativo/a	informative
preferido/a	favourite
polémico/a	controversial

Tipos de programas	***Types of programme***
el boletín informativo	news bulletin
el telediario	television news
el concierto	concert
el concurso el certamen	competition
el cortometraje	short film

el dibujo animado	cartoon
el documental	documentary
la entrevista	interview
el espectáculo	show, programme
el largometraje	feature film
la película	film
el programa de corazón	gossip programme
el programa deportivo/musical/infantil/ de debates	sports/music/children's/debate programme
el programa de telerrealidad	reality television show
el pronóstico de tiempo	weather forecast
la revista	magazine
la serie	serial
Las telenovelas	***Soap operas***
la miniserie	serial
la teleserie	televised series
el folletín	saga
el reparto del culebrón	cast of the soap
el/la protagonista	main character
el melodrama	melodrama
de carácter melodramático	melodramatic in character
el suspense (*Sp*) el suspenso (*LAm*)	suspense
los relatos románticos	romantic stories
una historia de narcos	a story about drug dealers
un asunto del corazón	an affair of the heart
la sentimentalidad	sentimentality
la exageración	exaggeration
la cursilería	vulgarity, affectation
conmoverse enternecerse	to be moved/touched
la acción	action
una gran cantidad de episodios	a great number of episodes
lleno/a de intrigas y engaños	full of intrigue and deceit
los argumentos enrollados	convoluted arguments
el final feliz	happy ending
la escasa calidad artística	low artistic quality
el programa más visto	the most watched programme
en su tercera temporada	in its third season

Los medios de comunicación escritos y en Internet

The media in writing and on the internet

Vocabulario clave	***Key vocabulary***
los medios de comunicación	media
el medio	medium
mediático/a	(of the) media
el periódico	newspaper
el diario	daily paper
la revista semanal/mensual	weekly/monthly magazine
la portada	cover page
los titulares	headlines
el artículo	article
el/la lector(a)	reader
el ordenador (*Sp*) la computadora (*LAm*)	computer
Internet (*usually without definite article*)	internet
el portátil	laptop
en línea	online
la red	web, internet
el enlace	link
la aplicación (app)	application (app)
chatear	to chat
la red social	social network
el móvil (*Sp*) el celular (*LAm*)	mobile phone
el teléfono inteligente	smartphone
el usuario	user

La prensa	***The press***
la revista deportiva/futbolística	sports/football magazine
la prensa amarilla/sensacionalista	gutter press
la revista/prensa del corazón	glossy, romantic magazine/press
la prensa rosa	gossip magazines
el periódico sensacionalista el tabloide	tabloid
el semanario	weekly newspaper
la circulación	circulation
el/la periodista	journalist

el/la reportero/a	reporter
el/la redactor(a)	editor
redactar un periódico	to edit a newspaper
las noticias de economía/deportes	economic/sports news
el artículo de fondo	editorial article
la reseña	review
el triunfo	scoop
la consultora sentimental	agony aunt
la columna de chismes	gossip column
defender la libertad de la prensa	to defend the freedom of the press
ser partidario/a de	to be biased in favour of
el juicio parcial	biased judgement
apoyar una opinión política	to support a political opinion
invadir la intimidad de alguien	to invade somebody's privacy
informar del acontecer diario	to report on daily events
publicar noticias y temas de actualidad	to publish news and current affairs
informar sobre la vida de los famosos/la moda/los deportes/la cultura	to report on famous people/fashion/sport/culture
poner al corriente	to bring up to date
actualizar	to update
la actualización la puesta al día	update
informar sobre los acontecimientos recientes	to report on recent events
la digitalización de los medios	digitisation of the media
los medios digitales	digital media
la fuente de información	source of information
la fuente fiable	reliable source
la columna de opinión	opinión column
enterarse de lo que pasa en la política/el mundo	to find out about what is going in on in politics/the world
informar de lo que sucede a nivel político	to report on what is happening in politics
publicar la actualidad política	to publish current political events
una revista famosa por el cotilleo que publica	a magazine famous for the gossip it publishes

Internet	***The internet***
el correo electrónico el e-mail	e-mail

la dirección de correo electrónico	e-mail address
mandar por correo electrónico	to send by e-mail, to e-mail
conectarse con	to connect/link up with
el video llamada	video call
la conexión de redes	networking
tener acceso a un chat	to have access to a chat
el salón de chateo	chatroom
el/la seguidor(a)	follower
compartir	to share
la cuenta	account
la red de amigos	network of friends
compartir noticias	to share news (ítems)
comunicarse	to communicate
el/la bloguero/a	blogger
entrar en contacto con un grupo	to get into contact with a group
los contactos favoritos	favourite contacts
el perfil	profile
crear un perfil	to build a profile
solicitar	to request
el/la emisor(a) de un mensaje	sender of a message
el/la receptor(a) de un mensaje	receiver of a message
enviar	to send
etiquetar imágenes	to tag pictures
interactuar	to interact
intercambiar	to exchange
interconectar	to interconnect
ligar en línea	to flirt online
publicar imágenes	to publish images
la foto	photo
postear una foto subir una foto	to post/upload a photo
socializar en línea	to socialise online
las citas en línea	online dating
tuittear	to tweet
en tiempo real	in real time
vincular	to link

El impacto en la sociedad y la política — *Impact on society and politics*

Vocabulario clave	***Key vocabulary***
influenciar / influir	to influence
la influencia / el influjo	influence
los medios de comunicación visuales	the visual media
la prensa escrita	print media
controlar los medios de comunicación	to control the media
estar al día	to be up to date
promocionar una marca	to promote a brand
formar valores/modos de vida	to shape values/ways of life
formar la opinión pública	to shape public opinion

El impacto de la televisión	***Impact of television***
el influjo sobre los valores morales	influence on moral values
ejercer una gran influencia en los televidentes	to exercise a great influence on viewers
informar a los telespectadores de las últimas noticias	to inform viewers of the latest news
la noticia de última hora	breaking news
las últimas noticias	latest news
una herramienta poderosa para educar a los jóvenes	a powerful tool for educating young people
una gran ayuda educativa	a great educational aid
aprender valores sociales de la televisión	to learn social values from television
proporcionar cultura	to propagate culture
ayudar a conocer otros países y otras culturas	to help to get to know other countries and other cultures
mostrar imágenes del mundo exterior	to show images of the world outside
ocupar los ratos de ocio	to fill free time
utilizar la televisión para no sentirse tan solo	to watch the television in order to feel less lonely

moldear/manejar a la gente a su antojo	to manipulate people as it pleases
una fuerza social destructora	a destructive social force

la relación entre ver violencia televisiva y la agresión en los jóvenes	the relationship between seeing violence on television and aggression in young people
perjudicar el desarrollo del niño	to prejudice a child's development
tener acceso al mundo de los adultos	to have access to adult life
contribuir a la apatía política	to contribute to political apathy

El impacto de la prensa escrita	***Impact of print media***
un punto de vista equilibrado	a balanced viewpoint
controlar los medios de comunicación	to control the media
el control de los grupos de comunicación	control of media groups
el poder de la prensa	power of the press
moldear a la sociedad	to shape society
el editorial	editorial
la columna de opinión	opinión column
denunciar abusos	to denounce abuse(s)
denunciar corrupción política/ bancaria	to expose corruption in politics/banking
la publicidad impresa	print advertising
el formato digital de los periódicos	the digital format of newspapers
el periódico digital	digital newspaper
La influencia de la prensa escrita disminuye.	The influence of the print media is diminishing.
la libertad de la prensa	freedom of the press
la libertad de expresión	freedom of expression
asegurar la salud de la democracia	to ensure a healthy democracy
organizar campañas de prensa	to organise press campaigns
revelar escándalos	to expose scandals
apoyar a los periodistas encarcelados	to support imprisoned journalists
denunciar las violaciones de la libertad de prensa	to denounce violations of press freedom
informar sobre:	to report on:
las convulsiones políticas	political upheavals
las transformaciones sociales	social changes
los cambios culturales	cultural changes
los escándalos bancarios	banking scandals
las campañas políticas	political campaigns
la vida de los famosos	the lives of famous people
adaptarse a las nuevas condiciones de los medios de comunicación globalizados	to adapt to the new conditions of globalised media

salvaguardar el derecho a la información de los ciudadanos	to safeguard the right of the citizen to information
la brecha informativa	information gap
la lucha entre el poder político y el poder de la prensa	struggle between political power and the power of the press
influir en el comportamiento de los políticos	to influence the behaviour of politicians
combatir la corrupción política	to fight political corruption
mantener una estrecha relación con el régimen político	to keep a close relationship with the political regime
influenciar las elecciones	to influence elections
la relación entre los propietarios de los periódicos y los políticos	the relationship between newspaper owners and politicians
un instrumento para movilizar a la opinión pública	a tool/instrument for mobilising public opinión
tener un impacto en el pensamiento y comportamiento de la sociedad	to have an impact on the thinking and behaviour of society
la falta de objetividad	lack of objectivity
el sesgo mediático	media bias
manipular las informaciones	to manipulate information
las noticias ficticias	false/fake news
publicar noticias ficticias	to publish fake news

El impacto de Internet	***Impact of the internet***
las redes sociales como una principal fuente de noticias/información	social media as a main source of news/ information
las redes sociales acercan al político al público	social networks bring politicians closer to the public
la rápida difusión de noticias a través de redes sociales	rapid dissemination of news via social networks
el acceso inmediato a información	immediate access to information
acceder a temas de actualidad	to access topical issues
volverse viral	to go viral
buscar información en Internet	to look for information on the internet
el acceso a la información	access to information
la sociedad de la información	information society
interactivo/a	interactive
Internet con fines educativos	the internet for educational purposes
la formación online	online learning
la formación a distancia	distance learning
la comunidad virtual	virtual community
el foro online	online forum

el intercambio de información rápido	rapid exchange of information
la autopista de la información	information highway
leer las noticias mientras caminamos por la calle/esperamos el autobús/hacemos cola	to read the news while we walk along the street/wait for the bus/stand in a queue
transformar la cultura humana	to transform/change human culture
transmitir e intercambiar información	to transmit and exchange information
bombardear con anuncios	to bombard with adverts
tener acceso a los bienes y servicios	to have access to goods and services
influir en los hábitos de consumo	to influence consumer habits

---

una nueva forma de expresión por las redes sociales	a new means of expression via social networks
una fuerza de liberación para los niños y jóvenes	a liberating force for children and young people
recuperar contactos perdidos	to revive lost contacts
ampliar sus círculos de amistades	to widen one's circle of friends
facilitar el contacto con los demás	to facilitate contact with others
conectar a gente sin importar la distancia	to link up with people irrespective of the distance
hacer amigos alrededor del mundo	to make friends all over the world
eliminar fronteras geográficas	to eliminate geographical barriers
enviar/recibir mensajes en tiempo real	to send/receive message in real time
conectarse velozmente	to link up rapidly
hacer videollamadas	to make video calls

---

hallar su camino a través del GPS	to find one's way using GPS
leer libros en línea	to read books online
localizar lugares/eventos de interés	to find places/events of interest
reproducir música	to reproduce music
sacar fotos	to take photos

---

aislar (a alguien) socialmente	to isolate (someone) socially
el aislamiento	isolation
convertirse en adicto al móvil	to become a mobile addict
la dependencia al usar un móvil	dependency on the mobile
el uso del móvil al conducir un vehículo	the use of a mobile when driving
estar expuesto/a a estafadores	to be vulnerable to fraudsters
compulsivo/a	compulsive
adictivo/a	addictive

estar enganchado/a a	to be hooked on
perder el tiempo	to waste time
perjudicial dañino/a	harmful
el ciberacoso	cyberbullying
abusar (de alguien)	to abuse (someone)
abusador(a)	abusive

el ciberdelito	cybercrime
el ciberterrorismo	cyberterrorism
el/la pirata informático/a el/la hacker	hacker
hackear	to hack
el virus troyano	Trojan virus
el aviso	warning
el ciberataque	cyberattack
la alerta sobre virus	virus alert
el antivirus	antivirus
eliminar un virus	to get rid of a virus
el control parental	parental control
chantajear	to blackmail
el chantaje	blackmail
la estafa	trick, scam
ser víctima	to be a victim
la poca fiabilidad de la fuente	unreliability of the source
los contenidos inapropiados	inappropriate content
crear una falsa identidad	to create a false identity
el fraude	fraud
quitar privacidad	to take away privacy
robar datos personales	to steal personal information

Websites

https://elpais.com/tag/telenovela/a

www.rtve.es/television (television programmes Spain)

www.rtve.es/television/tve-internacional/programas-series (TVE Internacional)

www.antena3.com/programas (television programmes Spain)

www.telesemana.com (Latin America)

A Escribe en inglés el significado correcto de los siguientes "amigos falsos".

1 el collar
2 el canal
3 divertido/a
4 el aparato
5 la antena
6 genial
7 el gusto
8 la desgracia
9 el concurso
10 realizar

Strategy

There is a wide variety of prefixes in Spanish, most of which derive from prepositions. In some cases, the preposition remains intact, e.g. *sobre* as in *la **sobre**dosis* (overdose); in others, there is a change of spelling, e.g. *entre* which changes to *inter*, as in *interracial* (interracial).

B Subraya el prefijo en las palabras siguientes y escribe el significado en inglés.

1 autorretrato
2 contemporáneo
3 controvertido
4 deslumbrante
5 embellecer
6 improvisar
7 inolvidable
8 interpretar
9 irreverente
10 representante
11 sobresaliente
12 transmitir

C Escribe el significado en inglés de los pares de verbos siguientes.

1 acabar/acabar de
2 acordar/acordarse de
3 dejar/ dejar de
4 guardar/guardarse de
5 ir/irse
6 llevar/llevar a
7 poner/ponerse a
8 volver/volver a

6 Los festivales y las tradiciones

Los festivales, las fiestas, las costumbres y las tradiciones / *Festivals, fiestas, customs and traditions*

Vocabulario clave	***Key vocabulary***
el espectáculo	spectacle, show
el carnaval	carnival
la corrida	bullfight
la romería	pilgrimage
el/la participante	participant
el traje	costume
el desfile	procession
disfrutar (de)	to enjoy
festejar	to celebrate
pasear	to go for a stroll
ir de tapeo	to go out to eat tapas
el origen	origin
la costumbre	custom
los fuegos artificiales	fireworks

La identidad	***Identity***
acostumbrar a (hacer)	to be accustomed to (doing)
compartir	to share
caracterizar	to characterise
la comunidad	community
una costumbre típica	a typical custom
el/la habitante	inhabitant
Su origen se remonta a…	Its origin goes back to…
influenciado/a por la cultura árabe	influenced by Arabic culture
el patrimonio (cultural)	(cultural) heritage
la manifestación cultural regional	regional cultural manifestation
orgulloso/a	proud
originariamente	originally
todo el pueblo participa	the whole town takes part
la provincia	province
la región	region
regional	regional
rememorar	to remember, to commemorate
representar	to represent

simbolizar	to symbolise
el refrán	proverb
el habla local	local speech
el dialecto	dialect
Los festivales	***Festivals***
a comienzos/mediados/finales de	at the beginning/middle/end of
la celebración el festejo	celebration
celebrar	to celebrate
el certamen	competition, contest
el festival	festival
la festividad	festivity
la cabalgata	parade, procession
la carrera de caballos	horse race
la carreta	cart, wagon
la carroza	float
la verbena	open-air party (usually nocturnal)
el cartel	poster
la entrada	ticket
el programa	programme
la fiesta folklórica	folk festival
el evento	event
el/la cantante callejero/a	street singer
la quinceañera	celebration of a girl's 15th birthday (Latin American in origin)
dar la bienvenida	to welcome
la concurrencia	attendance, spectators
los conocidos espectáculos	well-known spectacles
un espectáculo único	a unique spectacle

adornar	to decorate, to adorn
adornado/a con flores	decorated with flowers
la imagen (*pl* imágenes)	image
la iluminación	lighting
iluminar	to light up, to illuminate
iluminado/a por velas	by candlelight
alumbrar con velas	to light with candles
el tambor	drum
participar en un desfile	to take part in a procession
desfilar	to walk in procession/parade

el recorrido	walk, tour
salir a recorrer las calles	to go out and walk through the streets
el casco antiguo	the old quarter
crecer en popularidad	to grow in popularity
esta tradición atrae a miles de personas	this tradition attracts thousands of people
miles de personas acuden cada año a verlo	thousands of people go to see it every year

---

el ambiente de la fiesta	festive atmosphere
gracioso/a	funny, amusing
llamativo/a	striking, appealing
aplaudir	to applaud, to clap
divertirse	to enjoy oneself
la alegría	happiness
el jolgorio	fun, revelry
ir de juerga	to go partying
ir de marcha	to go out on the town
alucinado/a	amazed
animar	to enliven
destacar	to stand out
destacado/a	outstanding
fomentar	to promote

La ropa	***Clothing***
Los artistas visten típicos trajes.	The artists dress in typical costumes.
lucir	to sport (clothing)
el vestido	dress
la vestimenta	clothing
la chaqueta	jacket
el disfraz	disguise
la máscara	mask
disfrazarse	to disguise oneself, to dress up (as)
enmascarado/a	masked
llevar máscaras	to wear masks
salir a la calle disfrazado/a	to go onto the street in disguise
el traje tradicional	traditional costume
llevar una mantilla	to wear a mantilla
llevar puesto/a	to wear, to have on
vestirse	to dress
usar	to wear

Las fiestas religiosas en España	***Religious festivals in Spain***
la religión	religion
religioso/a	religious
la cofradía	brotherhood
la cruz	cross
el crucifijo	crucifix
la Cuaresma	Lent
la devoción a un santo	devotion to a saint
devoto/a	devout
Domingo de Resurrección	Easter Sunday
la ermita	hermitage
espiritual	spiritual
la fe	faith
fiel	faithful
el milagro	miracle
la misa	mass
la ofrenda	offering
los Reyes Magos	the Three Wise Men
Miércoles de Ceniza	Ash Wednesday
Viernes Santo	Good Friday
el Día de Todos los Santos	All Saints' Day
la Nochebuena	Christmas Eve
(el día de) Navidad	Christmas Day
las Navidades	Christmas (season)
navideño/a	Christmas
el/la penitente	penitent
el nazareno	Nazarine, penitent
la capucha	hood
descalzo/a	barefoot
el/la patrono/a	patron saint
la procesión	procession
rememorar la pasión de Jesucristo	to commemorate Christ's passion
rezar	to pray
el sacrificio	sacrifice
sagrado/a	holy, sacred
santiguarse	to cross oneself
santo/a	holy, blessed
reverenciar	to venerate
venerar a la Virgen	to worship the Virgin Mary

Las fiestas profanas en España	***Secular festivals in Spain***
la feria	fair, festival
festivo/a	festive

folklórico/a	folkloric
medieval	medieval
el paso	float (in carnival)
el muñeco	effigy
la hoguera	bonfire
el cohete	rocket
el petardo	firecracker
la pirotecnia	pyrotechnics
las campanadas de Año Nuevo	the chimes at New Year
las 12 uvas de Nochevieja	the 12 grapes for New Year's Eve
(la) Nochevieja	New Year's Eve

Algunos festivales tradicionales españoles	***Some traditional Spanish festivals***
el Carnaval de Las Palmas de Gran Canaria	Las Palmas Carnival (February)
las Fallas (de San José)	Fallas, Valencia (March)
la Feria de Abril	Seville Fair (after Easter)
las Hogueras de San Juan	*lit* 'the bonfires of St John', Alicante (24 June)
San Isidro	bullfighting festival, Madrid (May)
los Moros y Cristianos	Moors and Christians festival, Alcoy (April)
los Sanfermines	week of bullfighting in Pamplona (July)
Semana Santa	Holy Week (throughout Spain)
la Tomatina	tomato-throwing festival, Buñol (August)
la Virgen del Rocío	Procession to the hermitage at El Rocío to worship the Virgin Mary (Pentecost)

Algunas festividades latinoamericanas tradicionales	***Some traditional Latin-American festivals***
el día de los Muertos	the Day of the Dead, Mexico (2 November)
el día de Pachamama	indigenous festival to Earth Mother, Andes (1 August)
Inti Raymi	Inca festival of the Sun, Peru (24 June)
Feria de las Flores	flower festival, Medellín, Colombia, (beginning of August)
Fiesta de la Vendimia	wine harvest festival, Argentina (beginning of March)
Semana Valdiviana	traditional festival marking the end of summer, Valdivia, Chile (9 February)
las fiestas de Palmares	folkloric festival in Palmares, Costa Rica (January)
la Mama Negra	the Black Mother festival, Latacunga, Ecuador (September and November)

el Carnaval de Barranquilla	Carnival in Barranquilla, Colombia (week before Holy Week)

Algunos usos típicos españoles	***Some typical Spanish customs***
Es habitual picar tapas en varios sitios.	It is a custom to eat tapas in several places.
La gente acostumbra a comer en las terrazas.	People are accustomed to eating on terraces (i.e. pavement cafés).
el pincho	tapa
salir de tapas/de tapeo	to go out to eat tapas
salir a picar algo	to go out to have a bite
tapear	to eat tapas
hacer la sobremesa	to have an after-meal (lunchtime) conversation
el paseo	walk, stroll
tomar una copa	to have a drink
el mercadillo	street market
disfrutar de la vida nocturna	to enjoy the night life
dormir/echarse una siesta	to have a siesta
Los españoles se levantan pronto y se acuestan tarde.	Spaniards get up early and go to bed late.
Los horarios de las comidas son más tardíos.	Eating hours are later.
el puente	long weekend
la costumbre de saludar a la gente con dos besos	the custom of greeting people by kissing both cheeks

La tauromaquia	***Bullfighting (Spain)***
el capote	bullfighter's cape
el encierro	running of the bulls
la espada	sword
la fiesta taurina	bullfighting festival
la lidia	bullfight
lidiar	to fight
el matador	matador, bullfighter
la novillada	bullfight with young bulls
la plaza de toros	bullring
la sangre	blood
el toreo	art of bullfighting
el torero	bullfighter
el traje de luces	bullfighter's costume

Comer y beber	***Eating and drinking (Spain)***
el arroz	rice
la galleta	biscuit

la magdalena	cupcake, muffin
el pan con ajo	garlic bread
el pan con tomate	tomato bread
el pastel de hojaldre	filo pastry cake
el queso de cabra	goat's cheese
el queso manchego	sheep's milk cheese (from La Mancha)
el queso de oveja	sheep's cheese
la ración	serving, portion
la sopa fría	cold soup
el turrón	Spanish sweet, like nougat

---

el agua con gas	sparkling mineral water
las bebidas sin alcohol	non-alcoholic drinks
el refresco	soft drink
la cerveza	beer
la litrona	one-litre bottle of beer
la sidra	cider
el aperitivo	appetiser, aperitif
el vino blanco/tinto	white/red wine
el vino corriente/peleón	cheap wine, plonk
la denominación de origen	mark of origin (of wine)
el zumo	juice
la bodega	wine bar
el club nocturno	nightclub
la taberna	bar, tavern
la tasca	bar
la fiesta	party
la juerga	binge
vamos a tomar algo/una copa	let's have a drink
el bar de enfrente	the bar over the road
beber en la barra	to drink at the bar

Algunos platos y tapas tradicionales españoles	***Some traditional Spanish dishes and tapas***
los calamares a la romana	battered squid
el cochinillo asado	roast suckling pig
el cocido madrileño	Madrid stew
la crema catalana	kind of *crème brulée*
la fabada asturiana	Asturian bean stew
las gambas al ajillo	shrimps cooked in garlic
el gazpacho andaluz	Andalusian cold vegetable soup

las manzanas asadas rellenas de frutos secos	baked apples filled with nuts
la paella valenciana	Valencian paella
las patatas bravas	fried potato wedges in a spicy tomato sauce
el pulpo a la gallega	Galician-style octopus
la sopa de ajo	garlic soup
la tortilla española/de patata	Spanish omelette

Algunos alimentos típicos latinoamericanos	***Some typical Latinamerican foodstuffs***
el aguacate	avocado
la albóndiga	meatball
el alfajor	sandwich biscuit (Argentina)
la arepa	corn cake (Colombia, Venezuala)
el cacao	cocoa bean
el chile	chilli (Mexico)
la chirimoya	custard apple
la empanada	pasty, pie
la enchilada	*enchilada* omelette (with chilli peppers) (Mexico)
la fajita	Mexican tortilla stuffed with strips of meat
los frijoles	kidney beans (Mexico)
el maíz	maize
la papa	potato
el plátano	banana
la guayaba	guava (tropical fruit)
la papaya	papaya (tropical fruit)
la quesadilla	cheese omelette (Mexico)
el taco	maize omelette with fillings (Mexico)
la tortilla de maíz	corn pancake
la yuca	cassava (root vegetable)

Websites

www.spain.info/es/consultas/arte/patrimonio-mundial.html (https://tinyurl.com/yah8ubvs)

www.dodmagazine.es/festivales

www.huffingtonpost.es/2014/07/05/mejores--fiestas-populares-espana_n_5558017.html (https://tinyurl.com/ybyq5t9m)

www.spain.info/es/consultas/agenda/fiestas.html

http://guialocal.com/blog/es/2014/03/10/las-fiestas-populares-mas-famosas-de-america-latina (https://tinyurl.com/yaqvwsdr)

Strategy

A good way of extending your vocabulary is by linking words which have the same root. Think of words as being connected in families rather than in isolation, e.g. *cultivo – cultivar – culto – cultura*.

A Busca palabras de la misma familia y tradúcelas al inglés. Encontrarás algunas palabras de la misma familia en el vocabulario.

1 la costumbre
2 el pastel
3 al pan
4 la alegría
5 el vestido
6 el vino
7 el clima
8 la cocina
9 la cruz

Strategy

Prefixes are added to the beginning of words to adjust their meaning, for example *in* (*dependiente* → *independiente*), *de(s)* (*aparición* → *desaparición*), *sub* (*rayar* → *subrayar*), *re* (*poner* → *reponer*) and *tra(n)s* (*formar* → *transformar*).

B Añade un prefijo a las siguientes palabras para cambiar su sentido. Escribe la traducción de cada palabra en inglés.

	Traducción	**Con prefijo**	**Traducción**
coger			
dependiente			
diferente			
la esperanza			
gustar			
jugar			
la misión			

C Sustituye la palabra en cursiva por un sinónimo adecuado.

1 En España algunos dialectos están en peligro de *desaparición*.
2 Van a celebrar el *certamen* a las 11.00 de la noche.
3 ¿Cuál es el *significado* de "nazareno"?
4 El programa que vi anoche fue muy *gracioso*.
5 ¿Qué debo *vestir* para ir al festival?
6 En el *periódico* dicen que la fiesta comienza a las 3.00 de la tarde.
7 "Berenjena" es una *palabra* de origen árabe.
8 No nos atrevemos a correr ese *riesgo*.

Theme 3 Immigration and the multicultural Spanish society

7 El impacto positivo de la inmigración en la sociedad española

Las aportaciones de los inmigrantes en la economía y la cultura — *The contributions of immigrants to the economy and culture*

Vocabulario clave	*Key vocabulary*
el/la inmigrante	immigrant
inmigrar	to immigrate
el/la migrante	migrant
la oportunidad	opportunity
beneficiarse de	to benefit from
el permiso de residencia la tarjeta de residencia	residency permit
el permiso de trabajo	work permit
convertirse en ciudadano/a	to become a citizen
convivir	to live together
la comunidad	community
colaborar	to collaborate
la costumbre	custom
la diversidad	diversity
la aportación	contribution
la etnia	ethnic group
étnico/a	ethnic
el desafío migratorio	immigration challenge

Razones para emigrar	*Reasons for emigrating*
la esperanza de una vida mejor	hope of a better life
cumplir sus sueños	to make one's dreams come true
cumplir con sus expectativas	to meet one's expectations
una vida digna	a respectable/decent life
el bienestar	welfare, wellbeing

el reto	challenge
ahorrar	to save up
los ahorros	savings
las remesas migratorias	remittances sent home by migrants
La llegada	***Arrival***
llegar de fuera	to arrive from overseas
la llegada masiva	massive influx
el flujo de inmigrantes legales	flow of legal immigrants
recién llegado/a	new arrival
el país receptor	host country
la acogida	reception, welcome
el centro de acogida	reception centre
la solicitud	application
solicitar una visa/un visado	to apply for a visa
traspasar	to go through
tramitar	to process
el trámite	process, procedure
hacer trámites	to complete bureaucratic formalities
registrarse empadronar(se)	to register
el empadronamiento	registration (e.g. of residency)
el proceso de integración	integration process
La vivienda	***Housing***
asentarse	to settle down
establecerse	to settle
el domicilio	abode, home
el/la inquilino/a	tenant
cambiar de residencia	to move house
la inmobiliaria	estate agency
la hipoteca	mortgage
comprar vivienda	to buy a home
el préstamo	loan
la vivienda arrendada	rented property
las ayudas al alquiler de vivienda	(financial) help to rent a property
El estatus	***Status***
el/la ciudadano/a	citizen
la ciudadanía	citizenship
el derecho a la ciudadanía	the right to citizenship

el ciudadano de pleno derecho	full citizen
nacionalizarse / naturalizarse	to become a citizen
la naturalización	naturalisation
pedir la nacionalidad	to apply for citizenship/naturalisation
la concesión de la nacionalidad	the granting of nationality
nacionalizado/a	naturalised
el derecho de voto	right to vote
legalizar	to make legal, to legalise
el estatus migratorio	migrant status
solicitar un permiso de residencia	to apply for a residence permit
regularizar su situación	to make one's situation legal
residir legalmente en...	to reside legally in...
tener los papeles en regla	to be legal
el/la residente permanente	permanent residency
el permiso temporal	temporary permission
la igualdad de oportunidades y de trato	equality of opportunity and treatment
la clase social más desfavorecida	the most disadvantaged social class

La convivencia	***Living together***
la población inmigrante	immigrant population
integrarse en la sociedad	to integrate into society
vivir juntos	to live together
convivir con los demás	to live with others
vivir en paz	to live in peace
lograr la convivencia	to achieve coexistence
la coexistencia pacífica	peaceful coexistence
apoyarse (en)	to rely on
la red de apoyo	support network
ayudarse mutuamente	to help one another
la comprensión mutua	mutual understanding
entenderse entre sí	to understand each other
comunicarse entre sí	to communicate with each other
la interdependencia	interdependence
llevarse bien con los demás	to get along with others
juntarse	to join, to get together
unirse	to join, to unite
la unidad social	social unity
la participación	participation
participar	to take part
desarrollar lazos de amistad	to develop ties of friendship

la solidaridad	solidarity
la armonía racial	racial harmony
el bien común	common good
el/la vecino/a	neighbour
la buena relación con los vecinos	good relationship with neighbours
las relaciones de vecindad	neighbourhood relations
convecino/a	neighbouring
el trabajo en común	work done together
cooperar	to cooperate
la cooperación	cooperation
una actitud tolerante	a tolerant attitude
tratar	to treat
el tejido social	social fabric
acostumbrarse a un país	to get used to a country
adaptarse a	to adapt to
convertirse en	to become, to turn into
sentirse a gusto	to feel at ease
desenvolverse	to manage, to cope
la fusión	merging
el rasgo	feature, characteristic
las señas de identidad	distinguishing/identifying features
el sentido de pertenencia	sense of belonging
el valor	value; courage
la pertenencia a un grupo	membership of a group
la asociación de inmigrantes	immigrant association
respetar los derechos de los demás	to respect the rights of others
el respeto a la ley	respect for the law
la resolución de conflictos sin violencia	non-violent resolution of conflicts
aportar al conjunto social	to contribute to society as a whole
la dignidad de la persona	personal dignity

El empleo	***Employment***
la oferta de trabajo	job offer
tener derecho al empleo	to have the right to work
incorporarse al mercado laboral	to enter the job market
desempeñar un puesto	to carry out a job
ganarse el sustento	to earn a living
educarse	to educate oneself
instruirse	to be taught/educated
la formación	training
buscar formación en el lugar de trabajo	to seek training in the workplace

ver reconocido su éxito	to see one's success acknowledged
autodidacta	self-taught
los puestos peor retribuidos	lowest-paid jobs
la mano de obra barata	cheap labour
los vendedores ambulantes africanos	African street vendors
los vendedores de artesanía	vendors of handicraft items
la libre circulación de trabajadores	free movement of workers
la falta de reconocimiento de las cualificaciones de inmigrantes	lack of recognition of immigrants' qualifications
La cultura	***Culture***
el estilo de vida	way of life
la identidad cultural	cultural identity
la difusión cultural	cultural dissemination
fomentar una sociedad multicultural	to foster a multicultural society
enriquecerse	to enrich, to get rich
enriquecedor(a)	enriching
el pluralismo	pluralism
la multiculturalidad	multiculturalism
multicultural	multicultural
el reconocimiento de los derechos culturales	recognition of cultural rights
los vínculos culturales	cultural links
las relaciones interculturales	cross-cultural relations
la mezcla racial	racial mix
concertar matrimonios	to arrange marriages
el colectivo musulmán	the Muslim community
la minoría islámica	Islamic minority
la vestimenta	clothing
Las nacionalidades de inmigrantes	***Immigrant nationalities***
marroquí	Moroccan
ecuatoriano/a	Ecuadorian
rumano/a	Romanian
argentino/a	Argentine, Argentinian
colombiano/a	Colombian
alemán/alemana	German
británico/a	British
italiano/a	Italian
chino/a	Chinese
los inmigrantes comunitarios	residents from other parts of the EU

¿En qué industrias españolas trabajan los inmigrantes?	***In which Spanish industries do immigrants work?***
la agricultura	agriculture
el comercio	commerce
la construcción	building
la hostelería	hotel industry
la limpieza	cleaning
la restauración	catering
el servicio doméstico	domestic service

Las capacidades y las oportunidades	***Abilities and opportunities***
asistir a la escuela	to attend school
el/la alumno/a talentoso/a	gifted pupil
la capacidad de la adaptación	ability to adapt
estar bien motivado/a	to be well motivated
la capacidad de trabajo	capacity for work
ser trabajador(a)	to be hard-working
el reto lingüístico	linguistic challenge
tener aptitud para los idiomas/las matemáticas, etc.	to have a flair for languages/maths etc.
organizar su tiempo	to organise one's time
obtener resultados	to obtain results
conocer sus deficiencias	to know one's weaknesses
acostumbrarse a estudiar	to get into the habit of studying
la igualdad de oportunidades	equality of opportunities
integrar a los inmigrantes en el sistema	to integrate immigrants into the system
ampliar la formación	to broaden one's education
moldear a las generaciones futuras	to shape future generations

Las aportaciones económicas	***Contributions to the economy***
estimular la economía	to boost the economy
España se ha visto beneficiada por el influjo de inmigrantes.	Spain has benefited from the influx of immigrants.
la demanda laboral	demand for labour
confiar en la inmigración	to rely on immigration
generar riqueza	to generate wealth
la mano de obra cualificada	qualified workforce
la empleada del hogar	housemaid
la interna	live-in maid
la movilidad	mobility

la ganancia	earnings, profit
superarse	to better oneself
la iniciativa empresarial	business initiative
crear una empresa abrir un negocio	to start up a business
un negocio rentable	a profitable business
trabajar a destajo	to do piecework
invertir	to invest
la inversión	investment
los productos étnicos	ethnic products
La inmigración:	Immigration:
estimula la economía.	stimulates the economy.
ayuda al crecimiento económico.	helps economic growth.
tiene un papel esencial en la economía.	has an essential role in the economy.
ayuda a que las empresas crezcan.	helps companies to grow.
beneficia la economía a largo plazo.	benefits the economy in the long term.
hace que pequeñas empresas españolas continúen a prosperar.	ensures that small businesses continue to thrive.
cubre la escasez en sectores específicos.	covers shortages in specific areas.
trae a entreprenedores que comienzan nuevos negocios.	brings in entrepreneurs who start new businesses.
trae a trabajadores jóvenes.	brings in young workers.
Los inmigrantes:	Immigrants:
abren restaurantes étnicos.	open ethnic restaurants.
trabajan en sectores donde la oferta de mano de obra resulta escasa.	work in sectors where the labour supply is scarce.
cuidan a personas mayores.	look after the elderly.
pagan impuestos.	pay taxes.
contribuyen más de lo que se llevan.	contribute more than they take.
no son una carga para el sistema .	are not a burden on the system.
se integran socialmente.	become integrated socially.

Websites

https://elpais.com/tag/inmigracion/a

www.mequieroir.com/migracion-/latinos-hispanos/razones

https://jdimmigration.es/inmigracion-aspectos-positivos-y-negativos-para-la-economia (https://tinyurl.com/yatc4a5y)

Strategy

Nouns are frequently formed from verbs by adding an ending such as *-ión*, *-dad*, *- anza*, e.g. *inmigrar → inmigración*, *necesitar → necesidad*, *esperar → esperanza.*

A Escribe un sustantivo que deriva de cada uno de los verbos siguientes. Luego traduce los sustantivos al inglés.

	Sustantivo	**Traducción**
desconfiar		
establecer		
ganar		
legalizar		
perder		
proteger		

B Para cada una de las siguientes palabras escribe su equivalente en inglés, y luego su significado inglés más común.

	Equivalente en inglés	**Significado inglés más común**
abandonar		
agravar		
culpable		
desaparecido/a		
la formación		
incorporar		

C Busca palabras de la misma familia y tradúcelas al inglés. Encontrarás algunas palabras de la misma familia en esta sección.

1 la formación
2 digno/a
3 la diversidad
4 el empleo
5 la limpieza
6 pobre
7 la riqueza
8 el sueño

8 Enfrentando los desafíos de la inmigración y la integración en España

Las medidas adoptadas por las comunidades locales / *Measures adopted by local communities*

Vocabulario clave	***Key vocabulary***
la convivencia pacífica	living together peacefully
integrarse en la sociedad	to get integrated into society
arraigar	to put down roots
la población de acogida	host population
el barrio / el vecindario	neigbourhood
el municipio	municipality, township
el ayuntamiento	town hall
pedir apoyo	to ask for support
la red de apoyo	support network
prestar el apoyo	to provide support

En general	***In general***
el domicilio	abode
el desarraigo	uprooting
el choque cultural	culture shock
las reglas de convivencia	rules of co-existence
compartir	to share
una sociedad integradora	an inclusive society
la cohesión social	social cohesion
una mayor concienciación	a greater awareness
pedir la nacionalidad española	to request Spanish citizenship
los colectivos que conviven en la ciudad	the communities that live in the town
los matrimonios mixtos	mixed marriages
los barrios en los que conviven españoles e inmigrantes	neighbourhoods in which Spaniards and immigrants live together
tener trato con	to have dealings with
el sentimiento de pertenencia	sense of belonging
la población inmigrante empadronada	the registered immigrant population
los centros de culto de minorías	places of worship of minorities
la multiculturalidad	multiculturalism
Cáritas	Caritas (official Catholic charity)
vivir de la beneficencia	to live on charity

la limosna	charity, alms
las obras benéficas	charity
la organización sin fin de lucro	not-for-profit organisation/charity
la Cruz Roja	Red Cross
los bancos de alimentos	food banks
la población marroquí/subsahariana/latinoamericana	Moroccan/sub-Saharan/Latin-American population
la población magrebí/de Europa del este	population from the Maghreb/from Eastern Europe

Los retos	***Challenges***
enfrentarse a un nuevo modo de vida	to face a new way of life
la vulnerabilidad de los inmigrantes	vulnerability of immigrants
la exclusión social de los inmigrantes	social exclusion of immigrants
la precariedad laboral	job insecurity
la falta de puestos de trabajo	scarcity of jobs
la inserción laboral	entry into the workplace
acostumbrarse a otro tipo de trabajo	to get used to another kind of work
los edificios hacinados	overcrowded buildings
la carencia de viviendas	lack of housing
el problema de las personas sin hogar	the problem of homelessness
la marginalidad y la pobreza	marginalisation and poverty
la falta de vivienda a precios asequibles	lack of housing at affordable prices
la falta de educación	lack of education
carecer de redes familiares	to lack family networks
la reagrupación familiar	family reunification
la insuficiencia de recursos	lack of resources
la asimilación cultural de los inmigrantes	the cultural assimilation of immigrants
mantener unas buenas relaciones	to keep good relations
los conflictos vecinales	conflicts with neighbours
las precarias condiciones en las que viven los inmigrantes	precarious conditions in which immigrants live
el desconocimiento del idioma	ignorance of the language
aprender un nuevo idioma	to learn a new language
los altos índices de fracaso escolar	high school failure rates
el absentismo escolar	truancy
el continuo crecimiento de los flujos migratorios	the continual increase in migratory flows
los traficantes de seres humanos	traffickers of human beings

Las medidas	***Measures***
una red de asociaciones fuerte	a strong network of organisations
garantizar la buena convivencia social	to guarantee good social co-existence
la acogida de migrantes y refugiados	welcome of migrants and refugees
fomentar la cohesión	to encourage unity
mejorar la convivencia	to improve co-existence
promover el diálogo entre culturas	to promote dialogue between cultures
el/la mediador(a) intercultural	intercultural mediator
la mediación intercultural	intercultural mediation
trabajar con las asociaciones de barrios	to work with neighbourhood associations
el tejido asociativo	network of associations
fortalecer el tejido social	to strengthen the social fabric
dar apoyo con la vivienda	to help with housing
encontrar el alojamiento temporal y permanente	to find temporary and permanent accommodation
mediar en casos de desahucios	to mediate in cases of eviction
defender los derechos humanos	to defend human rights
luchar contra las desigualdades	to fight against inequality
acoger a los refugiados	to welcome refugees
ayudar a conseguir trabajo	to help to find work
la mejora de la educación de los niños de los inmigrantes	improvement in the education of immigrant children
las clases de español para la población inmigrante	Spanish classes for the immigrant population
organizar talleres y espacios de encuentro	to organise workshops and meeting spaces
los talleres prelaborales	occupational workshops
respetar la libertad religiosa	to respect religious freedom
distribuir comidas	to distribute food
proveer ayuda alimentaria	to provide help with food
distribuir productos esenciales	to distribute essential products
distribuir artículos de primera necesidad	to distribute basic necessities
organizar recogidas de alimentos	to organise the collection of food
atender necesidades básicas	to meet basic needs
evitar roces	to avoid conflict
actuar en situaciones de conflicto	to take action in situations of conflict
prevenir situaciones de riesgo	to anticipate situations of risk
intervenir en conflictos	to intervene in conflicts
luchar contra el radicalismo violento	to fight against violent radicalism
combatir a las mafias	to fight against mafias

La marginación y el aislamiento de los inmigrantes / *Marginalisation and isolation of immigrants*

Vocabulario clave	***Key vocabulary***
el aislamiento	isolation
aislado/a	isolated
la marginación	marginalisation, exclusion
marginado/a	marginalised
el hacinamiento	overcrowding
la inseguridad	insecurity
el prejuicio	prejudice
la inmigración ilegal	illegal immigration
el/la indocumentado/a el/la inmigrante sin papeles el/la inmigrante irregular	illegal immigrant
la Ley de Extranjería	Immigration Law (Spain)
repatriar	to repatriate
la detención	detention, arrest
la desesperación	desperation
sobrevivir	to survive

En general	***In general***
carecer de red de apoyo	to lack a support network
el/la ciudadano/a de segunda clase	second-class citizen
el desamparo	lack of protection
desconocer el sistema	to be unfamiliar with the system
la desigualdad	inequality
la desprotección	vulnerability
añorar su país	to miss one's country
la decepción	disappointment
desconfiar	to distrust
la incertidumbre	uncertainty
incomprendido/a	misunderstood
perder la esperanza	to lose hope
sentir rabia	to feel anger
sentirse:	to feel:
diferente	different
discriminado/a	discriminated against
explotado/a	exploited
impotente	powerless

maltratado/a	mistreated
vencido/a	defeated

La vida de los sin papeles	***The life of illegal immigrants***
la inmigración clandestina	illegal immigration
el/la indigente	destitute person
estar en una situación irregular	to be in an irregular situation
desaparecido/a	missing
estar discriminado/a	to be discriminated against
clandestino/a	clandestine, unregistered
pedir dinero prestado	to borrow money
el peligro	danger
la supervivencia	survival
padecer	to suffer, to endure
darse por vencido	to give up
el temor el miedo	fear
vivir en el miedo continuo	to live in constant fear
el miedo a lo desconocido	fear of the unknown
agobiado/a	overwhelmed
tocar fondo	to hit rock bottom
perder la esperanza	to lose hope
convertirse en víctima	to become a victim
la lucha cotidiana	daily struggle
buscarse la vida	to seek a way to survive
arriesgar la vida	to risk one's life
acabarse el dinero	to run out of money
mendigar	to beg
vivir bajo el umbral de la pobreza	to live below the poverty line
vivir en la miseria	to live on the breadline
no tener más remedio	to have no choice
esconder(se)	to hide
la vulneración de derechos	violation of rights
recurrir a las drogas/alcohol	to resort to drugs/alcohol
el cruce clandestino	illegal crossing
traficar	to traffick
el traficante	trafficker

La vivienda	***Housing***
el barrio desfavorecido/marginal	underprivileged/marginal district
el barrio marginal	marginal area

abarrotado/a	overcrowded
desalojar	to evict
las camas calientes	beds rented by the hour
alquilar por turnos	to rent in shifts/turns
la reclusión en guetos	confinement to ghettos
el arrendador	landlord
sin domicilio fijo	of no fixed abode
el elevado precio de los alquileres	high rent price of rental accommodation
el impago	non-payment
la bolsa de pobreza	pocket of poverty
la búsqueda de vivienda	search for a property
el gueto	ghetto
malvivir	to eke out a living
la persona sin hogar	homeless person

El trabajo	***Work***
la mano de obra barata	cheap workforce
el empleo de baja remuneración	low-paid employment
la explotación laboral	exploitation at work
la economía sumergida	black economy
los trabajos poco cualificados	jobs for unskilled workers
tener derecho al trabajo	to have the right to work
despedir por "no tener papeles"	to dismiss on grounds of illegality
el contrato precario	unstable job contract
el trabajo inseguro	insecure job
perder el empleo	to lose one's job
quitar un puesto de trabajo	to take away a job

La repatriación	***Repatriation***
el retorno forzoso	obligatory return/repatriation
deportar	to deport
la deportación	deportation
el centro de detención	detention centre
expulsar	to expel
la orden de expulsión	expulsion order

Websites

https://elpais.com/tag/inmigracion_irregular/a

www.elmundo.es/t/re/refugiados.html

A Mira las siguientes palabras, luego traduce las frases que siguen al inglés. ¡Las palabras tienen al menos dos significados!

1 **valor**
Quería decirle la verdad pero no tuve *valor*.
El *valor* del euro ha aumentado mucho recientemente.

2 **lazo**
No sé por qué lleva ese *lazo* en el pelo.
En mi familia los *lazos* que nos unen son muy fuertes

3 **centro**
En este *centro* tenemos una relación muy buena entre los profesores y los alumnos.
Madrid está en el *centro* mismo del país.

4 **competencia**
Este alumno no tiene *competencia* lingüística.
Hay una fuerte *competencia* entre las dos empresas para conseguir el contrato.

5 **materia**
En nuestro sistema educativo hay muchas *materias* optativas.
Los países africanos exportan muchas *materias* primas a otros continentes.

6 **clase**
Javier me da *clases* particulares de español.
La clase media está situada entre la *clase* obrera y la clase alta.

7 **cura**
El *cura* está en la iglesia recitando oraciones.
Están investigando una nueva *cura* para el cáncer.

8 **cielo**
Cuando salimos ayer el *cielo* estaba despejado.
Si ganamos será un regalo del *cielo*.

Strategy

A 'false friend' (or 'false cognate') is a word that looks like a word in English but commonly has a different meaning, e.g. *actual*, which means 'present' (in time). For a list of false friends see Section B.

B Escribe en inglés el significado correcto de las siguientes palabras.

1 la asistencia
2 el culto
3 el éxito
4 solicitar
5 la desgracia
6 el rendimiento
7 la oración
8 la carpeta
9 el idioma
10 avisar

9 La reacción social y pública hacia la inmigración en España

El enfoque político hacia la inmigración — *The political focus on immigration*

Vocabulario clave	***Key vocabulary***
la política de integración	policy of integration
la política de inmigración la política migratoria	immigration policy
tomar medidas adoptar medidas	to take steps
el desafío migratorio	immigration challenge
la legislación antiracista	anti-racist legislation
la ley	the law
el proyecto de ley	bill
legislar	to legislate
el derecho	right; law (study of)
el colectivo inmigrante	the immigrant community
el/la asilado/a	asylum seeker, refugee
ilegal ilícito/a	illegal
discriminar	to discriminate
la diversidad cultural	cultural diversity
la desigualdad	inequality

En general	***In general***
la política de igualdad	equal opportunities policy
el principio de igualdad de trato	principle of equal treatment
poner en práctica	to implement, to put in place
el papel preventivo del Estado	preventative role of the state
una carga para el Estado	a burden on the state
un paso necesario	a necessary step
agilizar los trámites	to speed up the red tape
el apoyo	support
combatir	to combat
condenar	to condemn
proteger	to protect
la protección social	social protection
la atención sanitaria	health care

el acceso a los servicios sociales	access to social services
la seguridad ciudadana	public safety/security
el país de adopción	adopted country
la participación de inmigrantes en el mercado laboral	participation of immigrants in the job market
el empleo temporal	temporary employment
el desempleo	unemployment
el perfil racial	racial profile
luchar contra el racismo	to fight against racism
el combate a la discriminación racial	fight against racial discrimination
la inclusión/exclusión social	social inclusion/exclusion
el derecho de reagrupación familiar	right of family reunification
el derecho de culto	right of worship
el censo	census
la minoría étnica	ethnic minority
de raza mixta	of mixed race
el/la mestizo/a	person of mixed race
afrocaribeño/a	Afro-Caribbean
andino/a	from the Andes
latinoamericano/a	Latin-American
magrebí	person from the Maghreb
subsahariano/a	sub-Saharan
el país no comunitario	non-EU country
el convenio bilateral	two-way agreement

Los problemas	***Problems***
la disminución de la población nativa	decline of the native population
el proceso de envejecimiento de la población nativa	ageing of the native population
la entrada masiva de inmigrantes	huge influx of immigrants
la concentración de los inmigrantes en determinadas regiones	concentration of immigrants in certain regions
la escasa cualificación profesional de los inmigrantes	low occupational qualifications of immigrants
el frenazo de actividad económica	downturn in economic activity
la tasa de paro	unemployment rate
la precariedad laboral	job insecurity
la empleabilidad a largo plazo de los inmigrantes poco cualificados	long-term employability of low-skilled immigrants
la discriminación hacia las personas de piel negra	discrimination against black people

el rechazo de los inmigrantes por parte de la opinión pública	rejection of immigrants by part of public opinion
los roces con la población residente	friction with the resident population
la integración en el sistema educativo	integration into the school system
la escolarización de los niños de inmigrantes	schooling of immigrant children
el creciente número de hijos de inmigrantes	rising number of children of immigrants
los gastos sobre la educación de inmigrantes	expenditure on the education of immigrants
la transición de la escuela al empleo	transition from school to work
la identidad cultural de los inmigrantes	cultural identity of immigrants
la falta de destrezas lingüísticas	lack of language skills
el endurecimiento de las políticas de inmigración	hardening of immigration policies
la inmigración incontrolada	uncontrolled immigration
los indocumentados	illegal immigrants
la llegada irregular de personas por la frontera de Ceuta y Melilla	irregular arrival of people via the Ceuta and Melilla frontiers (two Spanish enclaves in North Africa)

Las soluciones	***Solutions***
Para resolver los problemas, las autoridades deben:	To resolve the problems the authorites must:
regular la inmigración.	regulate immigration.
conseguir la integración de la población inmigrante.	achieve the integration of the immigrant population.
acelerar el proceso integrador.	speed up the process of integration.
reducir las desigualdades entre la población inmigrante y la autóctona.	reduce inequalities between the immigrant and the native populations.
velar para que se respete los derechos humanos.	ensure that human rights are respected
promover la convivencia pacífica.	promote peaceful coexistence.
reconocer los derechos de los inmigrantes.	recognise the rights of residents.
hacer frente a las expresiones de racismo.	confront expressions of racism.
penalizar actos discriminatorios.	punish discriminatory acts.
establecer condiciones para la permanencia.	establish conditions for permanent residency.

crear trabajo.	create work.
limitar la entrada de inmigrantes ilegales.	limit the entry of illegal immigrants.

Las medidas	***Measures***
la reglamentación	regulations
las medidas a corto/mediano/largo plazo	short-/médium-/long-term measures
tomar medidas firmes	to take strong action
una campaña de concienciación	an awareness-raising campaign
el establecimiento de la cohesión social	establishment of social cohesion
la asimilación de los inmigrantes en la sociedad	assimilation of immigrants into society
la discriminación positiva	positive discrimination
la eliminación de la discriminación racial	elimination of racial discrimination
la vigilancia del racismo	monitoring of racism
establecer mecanismos para erradicar el racismo	to establish mechanisms to eradicate racism
investigar las denuncias de malos tratos	to investigate reports of abuse
facilitar el acceso de asilo	to facilitate access to asylum
poner fin a los desalojos forzosos	to put an end to forced evictions
proteger los derechos humanos	to protect human rights
garantizar los derechos humanos de los inmigrantes	to guarantee the human rights of immigrants
promover la igualdad de oportunidades	to promote equal opportunities
crear organismos dedicados a la igualdad	to create bodies dedicated to equality
erradicar el uso de perfiles raciales	to eradicate the use of racial profiling
penalizar la contratación ilegal de mano de obra	to punish illegal hiring of labour
garantizar el derecho a la salud/la educación	to guarantee the right to health/ education
acabar con la existencia de las escuelas gueto	to abolish ghetto schools

La legislación	***Legislation***
la propuesta de ley	proposed law, draft bill
el juicio	judgement, trial
el proceso	trial; process

juzgar	to judge
sentenciar	to sentence
la sentencia	sentence
la pena	punishment, sentence
la normativa	rules, regulations
perjudicar	to harm, to damage
la multa	fine
amparar	to protect, to safeguard
sancionar	to punish, to sanction
el principio de igualdad de trato	principle of equality of treatment
la igualdad ante la ley	equality before the law
el acceso de las minorías a la justicia	access of minorities to justice
el delito punible conforme a la ley	offence punishable by law
el Defensor del Pueblo	Ombudsman
el Código Penal	Penal Code
Ley de Asilo	Law of Asylum
Ley de Extranjería	Immigration Act
Ley de Igualdad de Trato	Law for the Equality of Treatment
Ley contra la Violencia, el Racismo, la Xenofobia y la Intolerancia en el Deporte	Law against violence, racism, xenophobia and intolerance in sport
erradicar la violencia del deporte	to eradicate violence in sport
sancionar cualquier manifestación violenta en el deporte	to punish any demonstration of violence in sport
prohibir pancartas que contengan mensajes intimidatorios	to ban placards containing intimidatory messages
La legislación antiracista castiga a los que:	Anti-racist legislation punishes those who:
menosprecian los derechos de las personas.	disregard people's rights.
incitan al odio racial.	incite racial hatred.
cometen un delito por motivos racistas.	commit a racially motivated crime.
atentan contra la dignidad de un empleado.	violate the dignity of an employee.
discriminan en el empleo por motivos racistas.	discriminate at work for racial reasons.
difunden ideas basadas en la superioridad racial.	disseminate ideas based on racial superiority.
financian las actividades racistas	finance racist activities.
Las leyes antiracistas:	Antiracist laws:
enfrentan al racismo.	confront racism.
fomentan la igualdad.	promote equality.

protegen las víctimas del racismo.	protect victims of racism.
intentan garantizar derechos.	try to guarantee rights.
prohíben la propaganda racista.	prohibit racist propaganda.
combaten los prejuicios que conduzcan a la discriminación racial.	tackle prejudices that lead to racial discrimination.
eliminan las diferentes formas de discriminación racial.	eliminate different kinds of racial discrimination.
protegen los derechos de inmigrantes en el lugar de trabajo.	protect the rights of immigrants in the workplace
buscan erradicar las conductas racistas.	seek to eradicate racist behaviour.
condenan toda distinción basada en la raza.	condemn all discrimination based on race.
prohíben por ley el uso de los perfiles raciales.	ban racial profiling by law.
sancionan las conductas de discriminación.	punish discriminatory behaviour
protegen la igualdad de trato	protect equality of treatment.
ponen freno a la discriminación por motivos raciales.	curb racially motivated discrimination.

La educación	***Education***
el papel de la educación	role of education
la educación multicultural	multicultural education
la escolarización de los hijos de minorías étnicas	schooling of children of ethnic minorities
la interacción entre culturas distintas	interaction between different cultures
la integración lingüística de los inmigrantes	linguistic integration of immigrants
enseñar a los niños acerca del racismo	to teach children about racism
celebrar la historia multicultural	to celebrate multicultural history
fomentar la tolerancia y la comprensión	to promote tolerance and understanding
promover la filosofía de la tolerancia	to promote the philosophy of tolerance

La opinión pública — *Public opinion*

Vocabulario clave	***Key vocabulary***
la (in)tolerancia	(in)tolerance
(in)tolerante	(in)tolerant

comprensivo/a	understanding
acogedor(a)	welcoming
el aporte cultural	cultural contribution
convivir	to live together
la discriminación	discrimination
el temor el miedo	fear
la xenofobia	xenophobia
el racismo	racism
el odio	hatred

En general	***In general***
lidiar con un problema	to deal/wrestle with a problem
merecer	to deserve
la convivencia	co-existence
el ciudadano de pleno derecho	full citizen
mantener la identidad cultural	to preserve one's cultural identity
el asesoramiento legal	legal advice
los derechos humanos	human rights
la mano de obra	work force
la tasa de natalidad	birth rate
las desigualdades raciales	racial inequalities
el color de la piel	the colour of one's skin
el/la mulato/a	mulatto
una actitud ambivalente	an ambivalent attitude

Las actitudes positivas	***Positive attitudes***
acoger	to take in, to accept
apreciar	to value, to appreciate
dar la bienvenida	to welcome
hacer sentir a uno bienvenido/a	to make someone feel welcome
ser comprensivo/a	to be understanding
ayudarse mutuamente	to help one another
prestar asistencia	to provide help
por caridad	out of charity
apoyar	to support
cuidar	to look after
compartir	to share
la capacidad de vivir juntos	ability to live together
la solidaridad	solidarity
tratar como iguales	to treat as equals

la organización benéfica	charity
aperturista	progressive, liberal
la asistencia humanitaria	humanitarian aid
el respeto a la ley	respect for the law
la campaña antiracista	anti-racist campaign
el grupo antiracista	anti-racism group
Los inmigrantes:	Immigants:
apoyan el crecimiento económico.	support economic growth.
necesitan un empleo seguro.	need a secure job.
traen a trabajadores jóvenes.	bring young workers.
ayudan a que las empresas crezcan.	help businesses to grow.
son más propensos a trabajar en áreas innovadoras.	are more likely to work in innovative areas.
ayudan a mantener el nivel de vida de los países desarrollados.	help to maintain the standard of living in developed countries.
apoyan la economía de su país de origen.	support the economy of their native country (i.e. by sending money back home).
tienen derecho a una vida digna.	have the right to a decent life.
frenan el descenso de la natalidad.	halt the decline in births.
contribuyen a aumentar la tasa de natalidad.	contribute to increasing the birth rate.
enseñan la importancia de la diversidad.	show the importance of diversity.
aportan riqueza cultural.	bring cultural richness.
aportan una variedad gastronómica.	bring a variety of food.
deben tener mejores condiciones de vida.	should have better living conditions.
Es importante:	It is important to:
aumentar la comprensión.	increase understanding.
crear un espíritu de entendimiento mutuo.	create a spirit of mutual understanding.
ofrecer protección.	offer protection.
derribar perjuicios	break down prejudices.
integrar a los inmigrantes en la sociedad.	integrate immigrants into society.
garantizar la asistencia sanitaria.	guarantee health care.
ayudar a inmigrantes a salir del gueto.	help immigrants to leave the ghetto.
terminar con la explotación de los inmigrantes	end the exploitation of immigrants.

evitar que algunos se deslicen hacia la marginalidad.	prevent some from sliding into marginality.
evitar la conflictividad social.	avoid social conflict.
poner fin a los mafias delictivas.	put an end to criminal syndicates.
combatir a las mafias.	fight the mafias.
crear mejores condiciones laborales.	create better working conditions.
ayudar a los inmigrantes a encontrar trabajo.	help immigrants find work.
preservar los derechos humanos.	preserve human rights .
abogar por los derechos de inmigrantes.	champion the rights of immigrants.
ayudar a los inmigrantes legalmente.	help immigrants legally.
considerar a los inmigrantes tan válidos como cualquiera.	consider inmigrants as worthy as anyone else.
salvaguardar la diversidad.	safeguard diversity.
apoyar los programas educativos a los niños inmigrantes.	support educational programes for immigrant children.

La actitudes negativas	***Negative attitudes***
la extrema derecha la ultraderecha	the extreme right
el/la extremista	extremist
albergar sentimientos racistas	to harbour racist feelings
el odio racista	race hatred
el comportamiento xenófobo	xenophobic behaviour
la hostilidad hacia los extranjeros	hostility towards foreigners
la conducta racista el comportamiento racista	racist behaviour
las acciones discriminatorias	discriminatory actions
el rechazo de lo ajeno	rejection of anything alien
el miedo al inmigrante	fear of immigrants
el miedo a perder su identidad cultural	fear of losing one's cultural identity
el miedo a lo desconocido	fear of the unknown
el temor al extranjero	fear of foreigners
despreciar a los que son diferentes	to reject those who are different
considerar a alguien inferior	to consider somone inferior
la superioridad de una cultura sobre otra	superiority of one culture over another
un prejuicio arraigado	a deep-rooted prejudice
fomentar el odio religioso	to stir up religious hatred
amenazar	to threaten

la amenaza	threat
amenazador(a)	threatening
el insulto	insult
burlarse de	to make fun of, to ridicule
el desprecio	scorn
un ciudadano de segunda categoría	a second-class citizen
la crueldad	cruelty
vergonzoso/a	shameful
abusar	to abuse, to take advantage of
echar	to throw out, to kick out
expulsar	to expel
humillar	to put down, to humiliate
injuriar	to insult
intimidar	to bully, to intimidate
maltratar	to abuse, to mistreat
rechazar	to reject, to refuse
vilipendiar	to vilify, to disrespect
Los inmigrantes:	Immigrants:
nos quitan el trabajo.	take away our jobs.
se mudan a nuestras casas.	move into our houses.
se benefician de las prestaciones.	receive benefits.
no hablan español.	don't speak Spanish.
participan en el crimen.	engage in crime.
mantienen sus costumbres.	keep their customs.
Hay que:	We have to:
reducir la inmigración.	reduce immigration.
poner fin a la inmigración ilegal.	stop illegal immigration.
imponer controles fronterizos más fuertes.	impose stronger frontier controls.
expulsarlos.	expel them.
tratarlos como inferiores.	treat them as inferiors.
prohibir el velo islámico.	prohibit the Islamic veil.
hacer que aprendan español.	make them learn Spanish.
apoyar a las fuerzas del orden.	support the police.

Websites

www.elmundo.es/t/in/inmigracion.html

www.abc.es/sociedad/inmigracion/

www.lavanguardia.com/temas/inmigracion

EXERCISES

A Busca un sinónimo y un antónimo para las palabras siguientes.

	Antónimo	**Sinónimo**
la tolerancia		
el odio		
legal		
combatir		
cruel		
expulsar		
acogedor(a)		
condenar		

B Relaciona los adjetivos siguientes con un sustantivo adecuado.

1. humanitario/a
2. agresivo/a
3. superior
4. violento/a
5. diverso/a
6. étnico/a
7. igual
8. marginal
9. saludable
10. legal
11. vejatorio/a
12. justo/a

Strategy

Nouns ending with the suffixes *-ista*, such as *racista* (racist), *deportista* (sportsperson) and *-nte*, such as *agente* (police officer), can be masculine or feminine in gender.

C ¿Cuál es el género de las siguientes palabras: masculino, femenino o los dos?

	Masculino	**Femenino**	**Masculino/ Femenino**
ley			
color			
hereje			
hostilidad			
brote			
perfil			
residente			
marginación			
inmigrante			
dignidad			
origen			
extremista			

Theme 4 The Franco dictatorship and the transition to democracy

10 La Guerra Civil y el ascenso de Franco (1936–39)

Franco y la Guerra Civil española — *Franco and the Spanish Civil War*

Vocabulario clave	***Key vocabulary***
el bando nacional	Nationalists/Nationalist side
el bando republicano	Republicans/Republican side
la sublevación	uprising
invadir	to invade
el enfrentamiento	confrontation
estallar	to break out (war)
la contienda	struggle
el ejército	army
las Fuerzas Armadas	armed forces
los milicianos	militias
los acontecimientos los sucesos	events
el triunfo	victory, triumph

La guerra	***War***
declarar la guerra	to declare war
emprender la guerra	to go to war
desatar una guerra	to unleash a war
cuando estalló la guerra	when war broke out
estar en guerra	to be at war
la campaña militar	military campaign
el conflicto	conflict
guerrero/a	warlike
una guerra sangrienta	a bloody war
prepararse para la confrontación	to prepare for confrontation

enfrentar	to confront
atacar	to attack
el ataque	attack
la agresión armada	armed agression
la invasión	invasion
luchar	to fight, to struggle
aplastar las fuerzas enemigas	to crush the enemy forces
el frente	front (war)
feroz	savage, fierce
el temor	fear
el horror	horror
sangriento/a	bloody
fusilar	to shoot
el fusilamiento	execution (by firing squad)
disparar	to fire (a gun)
lesionar	to wound, to injure
derrotar	to defeat
derrocar	to overthrow
vencer	to beat
mutilar	to maim
asesinar	to murder
el asesinato	murder
la destrucción	destruction
destruir	to destroy
perder	to lose
fracasar	to fail
denunciar	to report (to authorities), to turn in
triunfar	to succeed, to be victorious
la humillación	humiliation
el cerco	siege
rendirse	to surrender
la rendición	surrender
la cárcel	prison
el/la prisionero/a de guerra	prisoner of war
desertar	to desert
refugiarse	to take refuge, to hide
sobrevivir	to survive
el destierro	exile
la pérdida de vidas humanas	the loss of human life

recibir órdenes	to receive orders
la jerarquía militar	military hierarchy

---

la máquina de guerra	war machine
las tropas	troops
el cuartel	barracks
la flota	fleet
la Armada	navy
la brigada	brigade
la aviación	aircraft; aviation
el avión	plane
el bombardeo	bombing
el buque de guerra	warship
el tanque	tank
la bomba	bomb
el obús	shell
los armamentos	armaments
los suministros	supplies
participar activamente	to take an active part
el permiso	leave, permission
el servicio militar	military service
el aliado	ally

La Guerra Civil española	***The Spanish Civil War***
alzarse contra la República	to rise up against the Republic
sublevarse	to rise up, to rebel
tomar el poder	to seize power
proclamar	to proclaim
el pronunciamiento	declaration of a military rebellion
un acto ilegal	an illegal act
la legitimidad del gobierno republicano	legitimacy of the Republican government
las dos facciones en guerra	two factions at war
los vencedores y los vencidos	winners and losers
la lucha fratricida	fratricidal war
la lucha de clases	class war
el conflicto religioso	religious conflict
la persecución anticlerical	anticlerical persecution
"la cruzada por Dios y por España"	'the Crusade for God and Spain'
el bando triunfante	winning side/faction
las "hordas rojas"	the 'red hordes'

la Guardia Civil	Civil Guard (paramilitary police force)
el alzamiento nacional	the Nationalist uprising
el régimen militar	military regime
el golpe de estado	*coup d'état*
los militares golpistas	military participants in the coup
la bandera española	Spanish flag
la burguesía	middle classes
el/la campesino/a	peasant
el territorio nacional	national territory
la lucha contra los sublevados	battle against insurgents
la intervención de las potencias extranjeras	intervention of foreign powers
los suministros enviados a los rebeldes por los alemanes	supplies sent to the rebels by the Germans
las postrimerías de la guerra	the final stages of the war

El ascenso de Franco	***The rise of Franco***
el levantamiento el alzamiento	insurgency, uprising
engancharse al alzamiento nacional	to attach oneself to the Nationalist uprising
el comandante en jefe	commander-in-chief
el líder indiscutible del bando nacional	undisputed leader of Nationalists
capitanear la sublevación	to lead the uprising
liderar	to lead
encabezar	to head
el nombramiento	appointment
proclamarse jefe de Estado	to proclaim oneself Head of State
las tropas moras	Moroccan troops
el cruce del Estrecho de Gibraltar	crossing of the Straits of Gibraltar
los aliados alemanes e italianos	German and Italian allies
el avance hacia Madrid	advance on Madrid
la Junta de Defensa Nacional	National Defence Junta
el salvador de la patria	saviour of the fatherland
el apoyo de los monárquicos	support of the monarchists

Sucesos clave de la Guerra Civil española	***Key events in the Spanish Civil War***
el alzamiento militar en Marruecos contra el gobierno republicano	the military uprising against the Republican government in Morocco (17 July 1936)
el triunfo de las fuerzas nacionales en el asedio de Badajoz	the victory of the Nationalists in the siege of Badajoz (14 August 1936)

la liberación del Alcázar de Segovia	liberation of the Alcázar (Castle) of Toledo (28 September 1936)
el nombramiento de Franco como comandante supremo del bando nacional	appointment of Franco as supreme commander of the Nationalists (27 September 1936)
el comienzo de la batalla de Madrid	beginning the battle for Madrid (8 November 1936)
el bombardeo de Guernica por las fuerzas aéreas alemanas e italianas	bombardment of Guernica (Basque Country) by the German and Italian airforces (26 April 1937)
el ascenso del general Francisco Franco a la jefatura del Estado	elevation of Franco to Head of State (1 October 1936)
la derrota del bando republicano en la Batalla del Ebro	defeat of the Republicans at battle of the Ebro (River) (25 July 1938)
la caída de Barcelona	fall of Barcelona (26 January 1939)
las últimas tropas republicanas abandonan Madrid	last Republican troops abandon Madrid (end of March 1939)
el final la Guerra Civil española	end of the Spanish Civil War (1 April 1939)

Los republicanos contra los nacionalistas	**Republicans against Nationalists**
Las fuerzas del bando republicano contaban con:	The Republican forces had at their disposal:
el Ejército Popular de la República.	the Popular Army of the Republic.
las milicias confederales.	federal militias.
las Brigadas Internacionales.	the International Brigades.
parte de la Guardia Civil.	part of the Civil Guard.
parte de las Fuerzas Aéreas.	part of the air force.
parte de la Marina.	part of the navy.
Las fuerzas del bando nacional estaban compuestas de:	The Nationalist forces were composed of:
la élite del ejército español (de Marruecos).	the elite Spanish army (from Morocco).
las facciones rebeldes de las Fuerzas Armadas.	rebellious factions of the armed forces.
los milicianos de la Falange.	Falange (fascist) militias.
parte de la Guardia Civil.	part of the Civil Guard.
parte de las Fuerzas Aéreas.	part of the air force.
parte de la Marina.	part of the navy.
los carlistas.	Carlists (Catholic monarchist group).
unidades enviadas por Alemania, Italia y Portugal.	units sent by Germany, Italy and Portugal.

Las divisiones en la sociedad — *Divisions in society*

Vocabulario clave	***Key vocabulary***
el odio	hatred
la conflictividad social y política	social and political unrest
dos Españas irreconciliables	two irreconcilable Spains
los contendientes	opposing sides
los sublevados	rebels
los campesinos	peasantry
los terratenientes	landowners
la cruzada	crusade

En general	***In general***
dos Españas en guerra	two Spains at war
la sociedad polarizada en dos bandos	society polarised into two factions
la polarización de la sociedad española	polarisation of Spanish society
las familias divididas	divided families
una profunda división en la sociedad española	a deep division in Spanish society
una guerra en torno a la idea de la nación	a war around the idea of the nation
una guerra de clases	a class war
Se enfrentaron los sublevados y los republicanos.	The rebels and the Republicans confronted each other.
Cada vez se distanciaron más la derecha y la izquierda.	The left and the right grew further and further apart.
una división de la sociedad a nivel social, político e ideológico	a division on a social, political and ideological level
el enfrentamiento entre comunismo y anticomunismo	confrontation between communism and anti-communism
el Frente Popular	the Popular Front (Republican side)
los defensores de la república	the defenders of the Republic
la resistencia del pueblo contra el fascismo	the resistance of the people against fascism
las filas de la izquierda	the ranks of the left
unos grupos armados de socialistas, comunistas y anarquistas	armed groups of socialists, communists and anarchists
las divisiones internas de la República	internal divisions of the Republic
un país dividido por conflictos internos entre las facciones diferentes	a country divided by internal conflicts between the different factions

el enfrentamiento entre los partidos de izquierda y sindicatos	confrontation between the parties of the left and the trade unions
los "rojos"	the 'reds'
las conspiración militar	military conspiracy
la ayuda de aviones alemanes	help of German planes
el alzamiento conservador	conservative uprising
el poder de los caciques	the power of local bosses
colaborar	to collaborate
el/la colaborador(a)	collaborator
traicionar	to betray
el/la traidor(a)	traitor
la traición	betrayal
delatar	to inform on

El bando republicano	***The Republicans***
El bando republicano contaba con:	The Republicans had at their disposal:
las fuerzas políticas de izquierdas.	political forces of the left.
el gobierno legítimo de España.	the legitimate government of Spain.
el Partido Obrero de Unificación Marxista (POUM).	the Workers' Party of Marxist Unification
los movimientos obreros campesinos.	peasant workers' movements.
los sindicatos marxistas.	Marxist trade unions.
la Unión General de Trabajadores (UGT).	the General Workers' Union.
la Confederación Nacional del Trabajo (CNT).	the National Confederation of Work.
la Alianza Obrera.	the Workers' Alliance.
los grupos sindicales revolucionarios.	revolutionary trade-union groups.
el Partido Comunista (PCE).	the Communist party.
el Partido Socialista Obrero Español (PSOE).	the Socialist party.
obreros, campesinos, braceros, jornaleros y anarquistas.	workers, peasants, farmhands, day labourers and anarchists.
gran parte de la aviación y la marina	most of the air force and the navy.
la ayuda soviética.	Soviet aid.
las tropas leales a la República.	troops loyal to the Republic.
los voluntarios extranjeros.	foreign volunteers.

El bando nacional	***The Nationalists***
El bando nacional tenía el respaldo de:	The Nationalists were supported by:
las fuerzas políticas de derechas.	the political forces of the right.
los altos mandos del Ejército.	the army high comand.
las tropas de África.	African troops.
los pequeños propietarios agrarios.	owners of small farms.
los campesinos propietarios.	landowning peasants.
la aristocracia latifundista.	the landowning aristocracy.
los monárquicos.	the monarchists.
la alta burguesía.	the upper middle class
la burguesía acomodada.	the well-off middle class.
la clase media católica.	the Catholic middle class.
Alemania e Italia, con barcos, aviones e infantería.	Germany and Italy, with ships, aircraft and infantry.
la Iglesia Católica.	the Catholic Church.
los obispos españoles.	the Spanish bishops.
las juntas de ofensiva nacional sindicalista (las JONS).	Councils of the National-Syndicalist Offensive (or La Falange, the Fascist party).
la oligarquía industrial.	the industrial oligarchy.
los sectores más conservadores de la sociedad.	the most conservative sectors of society.
los defensores de los valores tradicionales/de la Iglesia/de la propiedad privada.	defenders of traditional values/the Church/private property.
El bando republicano quería:	The Republicans wanted to:
repeler la invasión.	repel the invasion.
luchar contra el fascismo.	fight against fascism.
resistir a los insurrectos.	resist the insurgents.
defender la democracia.	uphold democracy.
movilizar a las mujeres contra el fascismo.	mobilise women against fascism.
Ciertos grupos izquierdistas querían:	Certain left-wing groups wanted to:
establecer una dictadura del proletariado.	establish a dictatorship of the people.
eliminar las clases sociales.	eliminate social class.
abolir la propiedad privada.	abolish private property.
El bando nacional quería:	The Nationalists wanted to:
derrocar el gobierno elegido.	overthrow the elected government.
establecer una dictadura.	establish a dictatorship.
restaurar la monarquía.	restore the monarchy.

sustituir la República por una monarquía.	replace the Republic with a monarchy.
volver a una sociedad patriarcal.	return to a patriarchal society.
rememorar el pasado glorioso de España.	bring back the glorious past of Spain.
convertir la Guerra Civil en una "cruzada".	turn the Civil War into a 'crusade'.
luchar contra el anticlericalismo.	fight against anticlericalism.

Las causas del conflicto	***Causes of the conflict***
los desórdenes sociales	social disorder
la anarquía persistente	persistent anarchy
las destrucciones de iglesias	destruction of churches
la legislación anticatólica del gobierno	anti-Catholic legislation of the government
la amenaza de autonomía a las regiones	threat of the autonomy of the regions
las huelgas	strikes
los anarquistas y la colectivización de tierras	anarchists and the collectivisation of the land
los asesinatos de guardias civiles	assassinations of civil guards
el antagonismo entre el capitalista burgués y el proletariado	antagonism between the bourgeois capitalist and the prolatariat
el resentimiento de los campesinos hacia los propietarios explotadores	resentment of the peasantry towards exploitative landowners
la falta de justicia social	lack of social justice
la desigualdad social	social inequality
las condiciones pésimas del obrero	dreadful conditions of workers
los salarios muy bajos	very low salaries
las clases marginadas	marginalised classes

Websites

www.elmundo.es/t/gu/guerra-civil-espanola.html

https://elpais.com/tag/guerra_civil_espanola/a

www.bbc.co.uk/spanish/especiales/franco/franco.shtml

http://elesperpentoverde.blogspot.co.uk/2013/04/el-ascenso-de-franco-al-poder.html (https://tinyurl.com/ybob7azm)

www.biografiasyvidas.com/biografia/f/franco.htm

A Busca un sinónimo y un antónimo para las palabras siguientes.

	Sinónimo	**Antónimo**
participar		
el poder		
apoyar		
el conflicto		
la rabia		

B Añade un prefijo a las siguientes palabras para cambiar su sentido. Escribe la traducción de cada palabra en inglés.

	Traducción	**Palabra con prefijo**	**Traducción**
el acuerdo			
el orden			
atar			
atacar			
parar			

Strategy

A number of common words derived from Greek which end in *-ma* are masculine in gender, e.g. *el panorama*, *el enigma*. Some words beginning with stressed *a* and ending in *-ma*, take the masculine article but are feminine in gender, e.g. *el alma*.

C Muchas palabras españolas terminan *-ma*; algunas son masculinas, otras femeninas. ¿Cuál es el género de las palabras siguientes?

	Masculino	**Femenino**
llama		
sistema		
problema		
ama		
lema		
crema		
fama		
programa		

11 La dictadura franquista

La vida cotidiana bajo la dictadura franquista / *Daily life under the Franco dictatorship*

Vocabulario clave	***Key vocabulary***
el franquismo	Francoism, politics of the Franco regime
el régimen (*pl* regímenes)	regime
el fascismo	fascism
fascista	fascist
la Falange	the Falange (right-wing organisation)
la censura	censorship
la represión	repression
el poder	power
el dictador	dictator
la dictadura	dictatorship
dominar	to dominate
en la época franquista en la era de Franco	in Franco's time

El régimen franquista	***The Franco regime***
el Caudillo	fascist leader (esp. with reference to Franco)
el jefe de Estado	head of state
el/la dirigente	leader
el culto a la personalidad	the cult of personaity
el orgullo	pride
anticomunista	anticommunist
autoritario/a	authoritarian
católico/a	catholic
cruel	cruel
despiadado/a	pitiless, ruthless
desvergonzado/a	shameless
dictatorial	dictatorial
férreo/a	strict
monárquico/a monarquista	monarchist
reaccionario/a	reactionary
represivo/a	repressive
totalitario/a	totalitarian

el bando triunfante	winning side
la proclamación	proclamation
proclamar	to proclaim
tomar el poder	to take power
ejercer el poder	to exercise/wield power
consolidar el poder	to consolidate power
gobernar	to govern
mantenerse en el poder	to remain in power
el aparato político	political apparatus
la autocracia	autocracy
la autoridad	authority
la ley	the law
la promulgación	passing, enactment (of a law)
falangista	Falangist
el/la fascista	fascist
los principios antidemocráticos del régimen	antidemocratic principles of the regime
un régimen de partido único	one-party regime
restaurar la monarquía	to restore the monarchy
la patria	the fatherland
la ideología	ideology
identificarse con el catolicismo	to identify with Catholicism
el apoyo de la Iglesia Católica	the support of the Catholic Church
la lucha al comunismo	fight against communism
la falta de una política de reconciliación	lack of a policy of reconciliation
el sentimiento patriótico	patriotic sentiment
crear un nuevo imperio español	to create a new Spanish empire
el águila imperial	imperial eagle
la bandera tricolor	three-coloured/tricolour (Republican) flag
el lema "¡Una, Grande y Libre!"	the slogan 'One, Great and Free' (*lit*)
una dictadura duradera	a long-lasting dictatorship

El impacto sobre la población	***Impact on the population***
a comienzos/a fines/a mediados de (los años cincuenta)	at the beginning/at the end/in the middle of (the 1950s)
el respaldo popular	popular support
la estabilidad	stability
el orden público	public order
la paz social	social harmony
la desigualdad social	social inequality

el atraso económico	economic backwardness
la austeridad	austerity
la autarquía	autarchy (economic self-sufficiency)
la autosuficiencia	self-sufficiency
la pobreza extrema de la población española	extreme poverty of the Spanish people
el sistema de racionamiento	system of rationing
la cartilla de racionamiento	ration book
la escasez de productos de primera necesidad	lack of the essentials
la escasez de alimentos	food shortage
los artículos de primera necesidad	basic necessities
pasar hambre	to suffer from hunger
la hambruna	famine
el estraperlo / el mercado negro	black market
La opresión política	***Political oppression***
el gobierno autoritario	authoritarian government
el régimen militar	military regime
las fuerzas de seguridad	the security forces
los tribunales militares	military tribunals
ejercer un rígido control político	to exercise a rigid political control
la dureza de la represión	the harshness of the repression
silenciar a los disidentes	to silence dissidents
la eliminación de las voces disidentes	elimination of dissenting voices
el abuso de los derechos humanos	abuse of human rights
la persecución política	political persecution
la prohibición de los partidos políticos	banning of political parties
perseguir cualquier tipo de disidencia política	to persecute any kind of political dissidence
el adoctrinamiento de la juventud/de la mujer	indoctrination of the young/of women
la víctima de la represión	victim of repression
la dureza de la represión	severity/harshness of repression
el campo de concentración	concentration camp
el decreto	decree
detener	to arrest
la detención	arrest
temer	to fear
castigar	to punish

condenar	to condemn
las condenas carcelarias	sentences of imprisonment
la cárcel	prison
encarcelar	to imprison
el/la preso/a el/la recluso/a	prisoner
los presos políticos	political prisoners
torturar	torture
sentenciar a pena de muerte	to sentence to death
condenar a muerte	to condemn to death
ejecutar	to execute
la ejecución	execution
las ejecuciones por razones políticos	executions for political reasons
las ejecuciones de los opositores del régimen	executions of those opposed to the regime
fusilar	to execute (firing squad)
el estado de excepción	state of emergency
la maquinaria represiva del Estado	the repressive machinery of the State
el/la opresor(a)	oppressor
las represalias	reprisals
la política de la venganza	politics of revenge
el toque de queda	curfew
la negación de los derechos humanos	denial of human rights
la ley marcial	martial law
inhabilitar	to ban, to disqualify
amenazar	to threaten
impedir	to stop, to prevent
sufrir	to suffer
padecer	to endure, to put up with
rechazar la democracia	to reject democracy
la prohibición de las huelgas	banning of strikes
la intolerancia del regionalismo	intolerance of regionalism
la represión lingüística	linguistic repression
la obligación del uso del castellano	compulsory use of Castilian
la restricción del uso de las lenguas minoritarias	restriction in the use of minority languages
marginalizar a las minorías del país	to marginalise the country's minorities
prohibir toda manifestación de la diversidad cultural	to ban all manifestations of cultural diversity
sustituir las banderas tricolores por águilas imperiales	to replace the tricoloured flag with the imperial eagle

colocar la imagen de Franco en todas las oficinas públicas	to place a picture of Franco in all public offices
borrar todo recuerdo de la República	to wipe out all memories of the Republic
llenar las calles de los símbolos de los vencedores	to fill the streets with the symbols of the victorious side
el proceso de Burgos	Burgos trial (1970)

La opresión de las mujeres	***The oppression of women***
la sociedad patriarcal	patriarcal society
el modelo tradicional de familia patriarcal	traditional model of the patriarchal family
los roles diferenciados para hombres y mujeres	differentiated roles for men and women
la mujer supeditada al varón	women subordinate to men
el dominio masculino	male dominance
el rol de las mujeres	role of women
el rol de esposa y madre	role as wife and mother
el arquetipo de la mujer recatada y sumisa	archetype of the demure and submissive woman
la domesticidad forzada	enforced domesticity
dedicarse a las tareas del hogar/al matrimonio/a la procreación	to devote oneself to housework/ marriage/procreation
la prohibición de matrimonio civil	banning of civil marriage
la Sección Femenina	'Women's Section' (of the Falange)

La censura	***Censorship***
la función moral	moralising aim
el guardián de la moralidad familiar	protector of the family morals
el adoctrinamiento	indoctrination
el censor	censor
censurar	to censor; to censure
controlar	to control
suprimir	to suppress
vigilar	to watch, to monitor
prohibir	to forbid, to ban
la prohibición	ban, prohibition
incautar	to confiscate
vetar	to forbid
el juez	judge
la propaganda franquista	Francoist propaganda
el arma de propaganda	propaganda instrument
el NODO	newsreel (run by Franco)

la censura cinematográfica	film censorship
los cambios de guión impuestos por la censura	script changes imposed by censorship
los cortes en las películas	cuts in films
el rombo	diamond (used to warn of scenes with adult content)
el doblaje	dubbing
los medios de comunicación	the media
ejercer control sobre los medios de comunicación	to exercise control over the media
la falta de libertad de expresión	lack of freedom of expression
controlar la libertad de expresión	to control freedom of expression
la prensa	the press
imponer una estricta censura de prensa	to impose a strict press censorship
la ley de prensa	press law
Las divisiones en la sociedad	***Divisions in society***
la división entre vencedores y vencidos	division between winners and losers
una honda división de los españoles	a deep division between Spaniards
la oposición clandestina	clandestine opposition
los soldados del Ejército republicano vencido	the soldiers of the defeated Republican army
los soldados republicanos supervivientes	the surviving Republican soldiers
subversivo/a	subversive
la conspiración	conspiracy
el maquis	maquis (resistance movement)
los sublevados los insurrectos	rebels
la operación guerrillera	guerrilla operation
una guerra de guerrillas	guerrilla warfare

---

el exilio forzoso	enforced exile
el destierro	exile
salir para el exilio	to go into exile
exiliado/a	exiled
el/la refugiado/a	refugee
el refugio	refuge
los refugiados republicanos españoles	Republican Spanish refugees

el masivo desplazamiento de españoles fuera de España	massive displacement of Spaniards outside Spain
verse obligados a cruzar los Pirineos	to be forced to cross the Pyrenees
el éxodo español hacia la frontera francesa	the Spanish exodus towards the frontier with France
abandonar el país por temor a perder la vida	to leave the country for fear of losing one's life
emigrar para tierras americanas	to emigrate to (Latin) America
el país de acogida	receiving country
el gobierno en el exilio	government in exile
la pérdida de una generación de escritores y políticos democráticos	loss of a generation of writers and democratic politicians

el descontento social	social unrest
la agitación obrera y estudiantil	worker/student agitation
la conflictividad laboral	industrial disputes
las demandas de los movimientos obrero y estudiantil	the demands of labour and student movements
las manifestaciones culturales contrarias al régimen	cultural manifestations against the regime
el movimiento clandestino de oposición a Franco	clandestine movement in opposition to Franco
las actitudes separatistas	separatist attitudes
la lucha a favor de la democracia	fight for democracy
la disidencia política	political dissidence
los partidos opositores prohibidos	prohibited opposition parties
el/la opositor(a) político/a	political opponent
el PCE	Spanish Communist Party
el Partido Socialista Obrero Español (PSOE)	Spanish Socialist Worker Party

Websites

https://brevehistoriahispanica.wordpress.com/2012/12/05/franquismo/ (https://tinyurl.com/yaojojzl)

https://sites.google.com/site/histmundialbach/espana-durante-el-franquismo (https://tinyurl.com/y8jo2aog)

https://html.rincondelvago.com/dictadura-franquista_2.html

A Busca palabras de la misma familia y tradúcelas al inglés. Encontrarás algunas palabras de la misma familia en la sección sobre la dictadura de Franco.

1 el dictador
2 reprimir
3 sangriento/a
4 la paz
5 autoritario/a
6 encarcelar
7 luchar
8 aislar

B Escribe un adjetivo que deriva de los sustantivos siguientes y traduce el adjetivo al inglés.

	Adjetivo	Traducción
el monarca		
la soberanía		
el poder		
la establilidad		
el símbolo		
el escándalo		
la corrupción		
el fraude		
el orgullo		
la tiranía		

Strategy

A number of common words are differentiated in their meaning only by their gender, e.g. *el cura* (priest), *la cura* (remedy).

C Escribe en español las definiciones masculina y femenina de las siguientes palabras que cambian el significado según el género.

	Masculino	Femenino
capital		
orden		
parte		
frente		
margen		
cólera		
radio		
policía		

12 La transición de la dictadura a la democracia

El papel del Rey Juan Carlos en la Transición / *The role of King Juan Carlos in the Transition*

Vocabulario clave	***Key vocabulary***
el monarca	monarch
la monarquía	monarchy
el proceso político	political process
el poder	power
el papel / el rol	role, part
la democracia	democracy
consolidar el poder	to consolidate power
el Jefe de Estado	head of state
el jefe de las Fuerzas Armadas	head of the armed forces
el franquismo	Francoism

En general	***In general***
tomar las riendas	to take the reins (of power)
el Tribunal Supremo	Supreme Court
juzgar	to judge
el/la consejero/a / el/la asesor(a)	adviser
el discurso	speech
el legado	legacy
el pueblo español	the Spanish people
el rechazo	rejection
encargar	to put in charge
el esfuerzo	effort
la cautela	caution, prudence
la lealtad	loyalty
instaurar	to establish
consensuar	to reach an agreement
destacar	to stand out
una fuente de conflictos	a source of conflict
la magistratura	judiciary
restablecer la democracia	to reestablish democracy
la voluntad de diálogo	desire for dialogue
el acto	act, ceremony

el sistema constitucional	constitutional system
el Congreso de Diputados	lower house of the Spanish Parliament
La situación política y social en España, 1975–76	***The political situation in Spain, 1975–76***
el sistema político heredado de Franco	political system inherited from Franco
la inestabilidad política	political instability
mucha conflictividad sociolaboral	a great deal of social-industrial conflict
el clima de enfrentamiento	climate of confrontation
las detenciones de líderes políticos	arrests of political leaders
la falta de libertad sindical	lack of freedom of trade unions
una oleada de las huelgas	a wave of strikes
la represión violenta de las protestas	violent repression of protests
unos manifestantes asesinados por la policia	demonstrators killed by police
los asesinatos cometidos por los terroristas de ETA	murders committed by ETA terrorists
el fracaso del gobierno de Arias Navarro	failure of Arias Navarro's government
un gobierno incapaz	an inept government
carecer del liderazgo necesario	to lack the necessary leadership
La monarquía	***The monarchy***
la corona española	the Spanish Crown
el rey	king
los Reyes de España	King and Queen of Spain
la soberanía	sovereignty
el/la soberano/a	sovereign
el jefe de la Casa Real	head of the Royal House
la jefatura de estado	headship of state
la dinastía	dynasty
dinástico/a	dynastic
la restauración de la monarquía	the restoration of the monarchy
Franco nombró a Juan Carlos como su sucesor	Franco appointed Juan Carlos as his succesor (1969)
heredar	to inherit
hereditario/a	hereditary
el heredero legítimo al trono	the legitimate heir to the throne

acceder al trono	to succeed to the throne
la proclamación	proclamation
proclamarse rey	to be proclaimed king
la coronación	coronation
el reinado	reign
durante el reinado de...	during the reign of...
reinar	to reign
el reino	realm, kingdom
el poder político del rey	the political power of the King
gozar del poder hereditario	to enjoy hereditary power
el Rey constitucional de España	the constitutional King of Spain
la relación con los militares	relationship with the military
desempeñar un papel clave	to play a key role
fortalecer la monarquía	to strengthen the monarchy
resolver una crisis	to resolve a crisis
cumplir con su deber	to fulfil one's duty
las obligaciones oficiales	official duties
el símbolo de la unidad de la nación	symbol of national unity
Su figura era una garantía de orden y estabilidad.	His figure was a guarantor of order and stabilty.

Las acciones del Rey durante la Transición	***The King's actions during the Transition***
El Rey:	The King:
vio la necesidad del cambio.	saw the necessity for change.
salió públicamente en defensa de la legalidad.	came out publicly in defence of the rule of law.
ayudó a diseñar un plan de cambio político.	helped to design a plan for political change.
renunció a la mayor parte de los poderes que había heredado de la dictadura.	gave up most of the powers he had inherited from the dictatorship.
se convirtió en un monarca parlamentario con poderes meramente simbólicos.	became a parliamentary monarch with only symbolic powers.
consolidó el régimen democrático.	consolidated the democratic regime.
impulsó una transición pacífica de la dictadura a la democracia.	pushed for a peaceful transition from dictatorship to democracy.
destituyó a Arias Navarro.	dismissed Arias Navarro.

asumió el proyecto del sector reformista.	took on the reformist agenda.
nombró a un joven reformista Adolfo Suárez jefe del gobierno.	appointed Alfonso Suárez, a young reformer, as head of government.
introdujo cambios graduales en las leyes fundamentales.	introduced gradual changes in the fundamental laws.
se puso en contacto con la oposición política.	contacted the political opposition.
estaba rodeado de un grupo asesores.	was surrounded by a group of advisers.
mantenía vivo el contacto regular con las Fuerzas Armadas.	kept regular contact with the armed forces.
actuó decisivamente para resolver el intento de golpe de estado.	acted decisively to resolve the attempted coup.
se ganó el respeto general dentro y fuera de España.	earned general respect inside and outside Spain.

El gobierno de Suárez — *The Suárez government*

Vocabulario clave	***Key vocabulary***
el/la presidente/a	president (equivalent to prime minister)
la Constitución de 1978	1978 Constitution
la Unión de Centro Democrático (UCD)	Union of the Democratic Centre (Suárez's party)
el Partido Socialista Obrero Español (PSOE)	Spanish Socialist Worker Party
elegir	to elect
gobernar	to govern
el partido centrista	centre party
derechista	right-wing
el/la derechista	right-winger
izquierdista	left-wing
el/la izquierdista	left-winger
el poder político	political power
el "tejerazo"	Colonel Tejero's failed coup (1981)

En general	***In general***
el éxito el acierto	success

el/la protagonista	protagonist, main character
conciliador(a)	conciliatory
el trato	deal, agreement
el riesgo	risk
la meta	goal, aim
darse cuenta	to realise
evolucionar	to evolve, to develop
instaurar	to establish
consolidar	to consolidate
lograr	to achieve
jugar un papel primordial	to play a key role
romper tajantemente con el pasado	to break radically with the past
dimitir	to resign

El gobierno	***The government***
el Parlamento	Parliament
la Cámara	Chamber
el Congreso de los Diputados	the Congress of Deputies (Spanish lower house)
la presidencia	presidency
el gabinete	cabinet
el partido	party
los máximos dirigentes del partido	top party leaders
el/la líder	leader
bajo el liderazgo de [x]	under the leadership of [x]
el gobierno encabezado por [x]	government headed by [x]
un gobierno de izquierdas/derechas	a left-wing/right-wing government
el ala (*f*) derecha del partido	right wing of the party
el comunismo	communism
comunista	communist
el socialismo	socialism
socialista	socialist
conservador(a)	conservative
los aperturistas	progressives
los reformistas	reformists
el pluralismo	pluralism
el/la político/a	politician
la política	politics; policy

el debate	debate
la polémica	discussion, argument, polemic
polémico/a	controversial
la oposición	the opposition
la crisis económica	economic crisis
celebrar	to celebrate, to hold (e.g. elections)
el escaño	(parliamentary) seat
las elecciones generales	general election
el electorado	electorate
el referéndum	referendum
el apoyo popular	public support
el mandato	term, mandate
la legislatura	term (in office)
el consenso	consensus
la competencia	responsibility
el planteamiento	approach
la propuesta	proposal
promulgar	to pass (law)
aprobar	to approve, to pass (law)
redactar	to draw up

Los retos	***Challenges***
llevar adelante el proceso de transición a la democracia	to carry out the process of the transition to democracy
pasar de un sistema político dictatorial a un régimen democrático	to go from a dictatorial political system to a democratic regime
crear una Constitución	to draw up a Constitution
atender las reivindicaciones de las regiones	to deal with the claims of the regions
los rupturistas	left-wing radicals (who wanted a complete break with the past)
los inmovilistas el búnker	ultraconservatives
las fuerzas de extrema derecha	forces of the extreme right-wing
el sistema político heredado del régimen anterior	political system inherited from the previous regime
sustituir las leyes fundamentales del franquismo	to replace the fundamental laws of Francoism
hacer frente a la crisis económica	to confront the economic crisis
estabilizar la situación económica	to stabilise the economy
los partidos políticos ilegales	illegal political parties

las conspiraciones golpistas	conspirators plotting a coup
la amenaza golpista	threat of a *coup d'état*
el golpe militar	military coup
los conflictos sociales	social conflict
desafecto/a	disaffected, hostile
la manifestación	demonstration
el paro	unemployment
el sindicato	(trade) union
la oleada de huelgas	wave of strikes
el Tribunal Supremo	Supreme Court
la magistratura	judiciary
el deseo autonómico	desire for regional government
las autonomías	self-governing regions
la Comunidad Autónoma	self-governing region (of Spain)
reconocer el derecho a la autonomía	to recognise the right to self-government

---

el/la terrorista	terrorist
el grupo terrorista	terrorist group
afrontar el terrorismo de ETA	to confront the terrorism of ETA (Basque Independence group)
ataques al ejército y las fuerzas policiales	attacks on the army and the security forces
derrocar el gobierno	to bring down the government
el atentado	outrage/attempt on someone's life
el asesinato político	political assassination/murder
amnistiar	to pardon
las negociaciones	negotiations
negociar	to negotiate

Las soluciones	***Solutions***
la Ley para la Reforma Política	the law of Political Reform
celebrar elecciones libres a unas Cortes democráticamente	to hold free elections to a democratically elected Parliament
desmantelar las instituciones franquistas	to dismantle Francoist institutions
iniciar contactos discretos con la oposición democrática	to initiate discreet contacts with the democratic opposition
crear un clima de consenso político	to create a climate of political consensus
la legalización de los partidos políticos	legalisation of political parties

firmar los Pactos de la Moncloa	to sign the Moncloa Pacts (agreed measures to deal with the economic crisis)
construir el Estado de las Autonomías	to build a state of autonomous communities
la aprobación de los Estatutos Vasco y Catalán	approval of the Statutes (of autonomy) in the Basque country and Catalonia

La Constitución de 1978	***The 1978 Constitution***
Rasgos principales:	Main features:
un estado social y democrático de derecho	a social and democratic state under the rule of law
la soberanía nacional reside en el pueblo	national sovereignty belongs to the people
el Rey como el Jefe del Estado aunque su poder es solamente formal	the King as Head of State but with formal powers only
una monarquía parlamentaria	a parliamentary monarchy
las Cortes elegidas por sufragio universal con poder legislativo	Parliament elected by universal suffrage with legal powers
un gobierno con poder ejecutivo	a government with executive power
el Tribunal Supremo, máxima instancia judicial	the Supreme court, the highest judicial authority
la descentralización del Estado	decentralisation of the state (allows for the creation of autonomous communities)
el derecho de hablar las lenguas regionales	the right to speak regional languages

El golpe de estado de 1981 — *The* coup d'état *of 1981*

Vocabulario clave	***Key vocabulary***
el intento de golpe de estado	the attempted *coup d'état*
la intentona golpista	attempted coup
el 23-F	23rd February 1981 (date of coup)
las Cortes Generales	Spanish Parliament
asaltar	to attack, to storm
el cabecilla	ringleader
sublevado/a	in revolt
conjurar conspirar confabularse	to conspire

el complot la conspiración la confabulación	conspiracy, plot
la crisis	crisis
fracasar	to fail

Los conspiradores	***The conspirators***
la amenaza de golpe de estado desde el Ejército	the threat of a *coup d'état* originating in the army
los tres protagonistas del golpe de 1981:	the three protagonists of the 1981 coup:
Antonio Tejero, coronel de la Guardia Civil	Antonio Tejero, Colonel of the Civil Guard
el general Milans del Bosch, capitán general de Valencia	General Milans del Bosch, Captain General of Valencia
el general Armada, antiguo preceptor del Rey	General Armada, the King's former tutor
un Ejército anclado en el pasado franquista	an army anchored in the Francoist past
los militares radicales de la derecha	radical right-wing soldiers
planificar el golpe	to plan the coup
el derrocamiento	overthrow
derrocar	to overthrow
la salvación nacional	salvation of the nation
la amenaza	threat
un golpe de estado que llevaba meses preparándose	a coup that had been months in preparation
los dirigentes de un golpe militar	leaders of a military coup
la sublevación la insurrección	uprising, insurrection
monárquico/a	monarchist
la salida de los tanques en las calles de Valencia	appearance of tanks on the streets of Valencia
los tanques rebeldes	rebel tanks
el cuartel	barracks
el toque de queda	curfew
alegar que estaban a la espera de las órdenes del Rey	to allege that they were awaiting the King's orders
el/la traidor(a)	traitor
traicionar	to betray
la traición	betrayal, treason

En el Congreso de Diputados	***In the Parliament building***
la investidura de Calvo Sotelo como presidente	the investiture of Calvo Sotelo as President
la toma del Congreso	the seizure of the Parliament building
un grupo de guardias civiles armados encabezados por Tejero	a group of armed civil guards headed by Tejero
irrumpir en el hemiciclo	to burst into the chamber
el enfrentamiento armado	armed confrontation
el asaltante	attacker
el revólver en mano	revolver in hand
tirar	to shoot
el disparo	shot
el grito de "¡Señores... todos al piso!"	the cry of 'Gentlemen… Get down'
tirarse al suelo	to throw oneself down to the ground
amenazar	to threaten
secuestrar	to kidnap
los diputados secuestrados	the kidnapped deputies/MPs
Las cámaras de televisión seguían grabando.	The television cameras continued to record.
desafiar	to challenge
enfrentarse	to oppose
el carácter inestable de Tejero	Tejero's unstable character
estrafalario/a	eccentric, outlandish
El golpe se abortó.	The coup failed.
fallido/a	failed
la rendición	surrender
entregarse	to surrender, to hand oneself over
A la mañana del día siguiente Tejero se rindió.	The next morning Tejero surrendered.
el/la vencedor(a)	winner
el alivio	relief
El papel del Rey	***The role of the King***
la intervención del Rey	the King's intervention
la actuación del Rey	the King's action
un discurso televisado a la 1.30 de la madrugada	a televised speech at 1.30 a.m.
vestido de general del Ejército español	dressed as a general of the Spanish army

El Rey:	The King:
apareció por televisión.	appeared on television.
se dirigió al pueblo español.	addressed the Spanish people.
condenó el golpe militar.	condemned the military coup.
defendió el sistema democrático.	defended the democratic system.
salvó la corona española.	saved the Spanish crown.
defendió la legalidad.	defended the rule of law.
resolvió la crisis.	resolved the crisis.
respetó la democracia.	respected democracy.
desautorizó a los golpistas.	disowned the perpetrators of the coup.
logró detener el golpe.	succeeded in stopping the coup.
abortó el golpe.	foiled the coup.
ordenó a todos los capitanes generales que permanecieran en sus puestos.	ordered all the Captains General to remain at their posts.
ordenó a Milans del Bosch que mandara volver a las tropas a sus cuarteles.	ordered Milans del Bosch to tell his troops to return to barracks.
hablar en su condición de jefe supremo de las Fuerzas Armadas	to speak as supreme head of the armed forces
la firmeza	firmness
la resolución	resolve
valeroso/a	courageous

Las consecuencias del triunfo de la democracia	***The consequences of the victory of democracy***
La intentona fracasó.	The attempted coup failed.
Se celebraron manifestaciones de apoyo a la Constitución.	Demonstrations were held in support of the Constitution.
un impulso importante para el sistema democrático español	an important boost for the democratic system in Spain
el refuerzo de la democracia	strengthening of democracy
Tejero fue condenado a 30 años de cárcel.	Tejero was condemned to 30 years in prison.
el fin del franquismo latente en los cuarteles	the end of latent Francoism in the barracks
El ejército se declaró fiel a la Constitución.	The army declared itself loyal to the Constitution.
el momento decisivo	turning point
el hito	landmark, milestone

Acontecimientos clave de la Transición	***Key events of the Transition***
la muerte de Franco	death of Franco (20 November 1975)
el acceso de Juan Carlos I al trono	accession of Juan Carlos I to the throne (22 November 1975)
Adolfo Suárez nombrado presidente del gobierno por el rey	Adolfo Suárez appointed to the presidency by the king (3 July 1976)
la aprobación de la Ley para la Reforma Política	approval of the Political Reform Law (November 1976)
la legalización de los partidos políticos	legalisation of political parties (December 1976–June 1977)
el triunfo electoral de la UCD	electoral victory of the UCD (15 June 1977)
los Pactos de la Moncloa	Moncloa Pacts (October 1977) (economic agreements to stabilise the Transition)
la ratificación de la Constitución	ratification of the Constitution (6 December 1978)
las primeras elecciones autonómicas (País Vasco y Cataluña)	first elections in the autonomous communities (Basque Country and Catalonia) (1980)
la dimisión de Suárez	resignation of Suárez (29 January 1981)
el intento de golpe de estado (el "tejerazo")	attempted coup by Colonel Tejero (23 February 1981)
el triunfo electoral del PSOE	electoral victory of the Socialist Party (28 October 1982)

Websites

https://elpais.com/tag/23_f/a

www.cervantesvirtual.com/portales/reyes_y_reinas_espana_contemporanea/juan_carlos_i_biografia (https://tinyurl.com/yb3yoenr)

www.rtve.es/noticias/20140323/dictadura-democracia-medidas-gobiernos-adolfo-suarez/900006.shtml (https://tinyurl.com/y99upkzo)

http://iris.cnice.mec.es/kairos/ensenanzas/bachillerato/espana/democratica_01_02.html (https://tinyurl.com/y8g4jese)

www.elmundo.es/especiales/23f

Strategy

It is important to increase the range of your vocabulary by learning synonyms.These words have the same meaning as other words, or are very similar in meaning to them, e.g. *apropiado/adecuado, mundo/globo, inhabitado/despoblado.*

A Sustituye la palabra en cursiva por un sinónimo adecuado y traduce las frases al inglés.

1. En el momento decisivo el Rey *apoyó* la democracia.
2. ¡*Lucharemos* por la libertad!
3. *A mi juicio,* Suárez no mereció perder la elección.
4. La mayor parte de la población catalana *acudió a las urnas* el domingo pasado.
5. *La encuesta* más reciente predice que los socialistas ganarán.
6. Le miró con *recelo* cuando ella reveló el secreto.
7. El mes pasado la tasa de *desempleo* descendió dos puntos.
8. No vas a *conseguir* hacer nada si no te esfuerzas.

B Relaciona los sustantivos siguientes con un verbo adecuado y traduce los sustantivos y los verbos al inglés.

	Traducción	**Verbo**	**Traducción**
la protesta			
la corrupción			
la percepción			
el poder			
el gobierno			
la elección			
la política			
el despido			
la dificultad			
la reducción			
la costumbre			
la riqueza			

Sección E

Investigación y presentación

The three additional vocabulary lists in this section, on Sport, the Environment and Fashion, are included to support you if you decide to explore one of these topics for your Individual Research Project, for the oral exam. Remember that your project must be centred on Hispanic society and culture and relate to one of the four themes: *The evolution of Spanish society, Political and artistic culture in the Spanish-speaking world, Immigration and the multicultural Spanish society* and *The Franco dictatorship* and *the transition to demoracy.*

E.1 Los deportes — *Sport*

Vocabulario clave	***Key vocabulary***
el deporte	sport
la actividad	activity
el/la deportista	sportsman/woman
deportivo/a	sports; sporting
el equipo	team
el estadio	stadium
el/la jugador(a)	player
el partido	game, match
ser deportista	to be keen on sport
el/la aficionado/a	fan
el/la entrenador(a)	trainer
entrenarse	to train
mantenerse en forma	to keep fit

En general	***In general***
el polideportivo	sports centre
los ratos libres el tiempo libre	free/spare time
las instalaciones deportivas	sports facilities
el/la campeón/campeona	champion
el campeonato mundial	world championship
los deportes competitivos	competitive sports
el concurso la competición	competition (= contest)
la competencia	competition (= competitiveness)
el deporte de equipo	team sport

proveer ejercicio físico	to provide physical exercise
la temporada de fútbol	football season
las competiciones europeas	European competitions

Los Juegos Olímpicos	***The Olympic Games***
las Olimpiadas	Olympics/Olympic Games
la ciudad anfitriona	host city
el estadio olímpico	Olympic stadium
el espíritu de equipo	team spirit
el juego limpio	fair play
las pruebas	trials
conseguir una medalla de oro/plata/ bronce	to win a gold/silver/bronze medal
batir el récord	to beat the record
el atletismo	athletics
el/la atleta	athlete
el/la corredor(a)	runner
la carrera	race
el maratón	marathon
el salto de longitud/de altura	long/high jump
el ciclismo de pista	track cycling
el boxeo	boxing
la gimnasia	gymnastics; gym

los Juegos Paralímpicos	the Paralympic Games
los atletas con discapacidades	handicapped athletes
los atletas con amputaciones	amputee athletes
el/la atleta con silla de ruedas	wheelchair athlete
el/la atleta con ceguera total	totally blind athlete
el/la atleta con parálisis cerebral	athlete with cerebral palsy

El dopaje	***Doping***
la amenaza del dopaje en el deporte	the threat of doping in sport
el uso de sustancias prohibidas	the use of banned substances
doparse	to take drugs
hacer trampa	to cheat
el fraude	fraud
la prueba antidoping	anti-doping test
recoger una muestra	to collect/take a sample
dañar la salud	to harm one's health
destruir el concepto de deporte	to destroy the concept of sport

afectar a los deportistas "limpios"	to affect 'clean' sportspeople
el impacto en los jóvenes	the impact on young people
Los deportes y el dinero	***Sport and money***
patrocinar	to sponsor
el patrocinio	sponsorship
los derechos televisivos	television rights
la estrategia publicitaria	advertising strategy
Los deportes son un gran negocio.	Sports are big business.
la ropa deportiva	sportswear
la avaricia	greed
ser rentable	to be profitable
Los partidos	***Matches***
tener lugar	to take place
participar (en)	to take part (in)
el resultado	result
el/la vencedor(a)	winner
el/la perdedor(a)	loser
la derrota	defeat
ganar / triunfar	to win
derrotar / vencer	to defeat
perder	to lose
la selección	team (selection)
la plantilla	squad
el/la adversario/a	opponent
el/la árbitro/a	referee, umpire
el terreno de juego	field of play
la liga	league
la copa	cup
el trofeo	trophy
el torneo	tournament
jugar bien bajo presión	to play well under pressure
el espíritu de rivalidad	rivalry, competitive spirit
fomentar el espíritu del equipo	to foster team spirit
chutar	to shoot
ceder un penalti	to give away a penalty
el ensayo	try
marcar un ensayo	to score a try

¿Cómo van?	What's the score? (game in progress)
¿Cuál es el resultado?	What's the (final) score/result?

Otras actividades deportivas	***Other sporting activities***
la natación	swimming
nadar	to swim
la piscina	swimming pool
bucear	to dive, to swim under water
zambullirse	to dive
el tenis	tennis
la pista de tenis	tennis court
el golpe	shot, stroke
el revés	backhand
el saque	service
el baloncesto	basketball
el esquí	ski; skiing
esquiar	to ski
el patinaje sobre hielo	ice skating
el patinaje artístico	figure skating
entusiasmarse por el esquí	to be mad on skiing
las pistas de esquí	ski slopes
dedicarse al ciclismo	to do a lot of cycling
la vuelta a España	cycle race around Spain
la hípica	horse-riding
apostar	to bet
jugarse el dinero	to gamble
los deportes de alto riesgo	high-risk sports
el senderismo	hiking, trekking
salir de excursión	to go on a trip
ser amante del aire libre	to be fond of the fresh air

Websites

www.mecd.gob.es/portada-mecd
www.marca.com
www.mundodeportivo.com
https://as.com
www.rtve.es/deportes
www.elmundo.es/deportes.html

E.2 El medio ambiente — *The environment*

Vocabulario clave	*Key vocabulary*
el entorno natural	natural surroundings/environment
el cambio climático	climate change
el recalentamiento del planeta / el calentamiento del globo	global warming
la deforestación	deforestation
la desertización	desertification
la central nuclear	nuclear power station
el ahorro de energía	saving of energy
despilfarrar	to squander
conservar la energía	to conserve energy
tomar medidas	to take measures
la contaminación	pollution

Problemas y soluciones	*Problems and solutions*
la amenaza a la naturaleza	threat to wildlife
el deterioro ambiental	environmental damage
la huella de carbono	carbon footprint
causar daños irreversibles	to cause irreversible damage
la supervivencia del hombre	man's survival
reducir los daños causados a…	to reduce the damage caused to…
el empeoramiento de la calidad de la vida	deterioration in the quality of life

Motivos específicos de preocupación	*Specific areas of concern*
el efecto invernadero	greenhouse effect
los gases invernaderos	greenhouse gases
la destrucción de la capa de ozono	destruction of the ozone layer
el agujero de ozono	hole in the ozone layer
el clorofluorocarbono	chlorofluorocarbon (CFC)
los hidrocarburos	hydrocarbons
el spray	spray, aerosol
echar/vomitar humos	to belch out smoke
los gases contaminantes	polluting gases
las lluvias ácidas	acid rain
la destrucción de las selvas tropicales	destruction of the rain forests
el derretimiento de la capa de hielo polar	melting of the polar ice sheet
derretirse	to melt

el aumento del nivel del mar	rise in sea level
con toda urgencia	with the utmost urgency
el movimiento ecologista mundial	world ecology/green movement
una catástrofe climática	a climatic disaster
la velocidad del recalentamiento del planeta	the speed of global warming
la utilización pacífica de la energía nuclear	peaceful use of nuclear energy
despertar a la opinión pública	to awaken public opinion
luchar por la supervivencia de las especies	to fight for the survival of species

Los recursos naturales	***Natural resources***
los recursos energéticos	energy resources
el consumo de energía	energy consumption
conservar los escasos recursos del planeta	to conserve the planet's scarce resources
Los recursos se agotan.	Resources are being exhausted.
el despilfarro	wastefulness, squandering
el aislamiento térmico	heat insulation
encender/apagar la calefacción	to switch the heating on/off
dejar encendidas las luces	to leave the lights on
los combustibles fósiles	fossil fuels
el petróleo	crude oil
la crisis de petróleo	oil crisis
sacar de la tierra	to take out of the ground
los adelantos técnicos	technical advances
la mayor fuente de energía utilizable	the greatest source of usable energy
los recursos renovables	renewable resources
el panel solar	solar panel
la energía eólica	wind energy
el aerogenerador	wind turbine
el parque eólico	wind farm
aprovechar la energía de las olas	to harness the energy of the waves
la central hidroeléctrica	hydroelectric power station
la hidroelectricidad	hydroelectricity
el apagón	blackout, power failure
la fractura hidráulica	fracking

La energía nuclear	***Nuclear energy***
radioactivo/a	radioactive
la fuga de radioactividad	radioactive leak

el siniestro nuclear	nuclear disaster
el reactor	reactor
la energía limpia	clean energy
montar una campaña antinuclear	to mount an anti-nuclear campaign

La contaminación	***Pollution***
La tierra, el mar y el aire	***Land, sea and air***
la basura	rubbish
el vertedero	rubbish tip
producir efectos tóxicos	to have toxic effects
contaminar	to pollute, to contaminate
los contaminantes atmosféricos	atmospheric pollutants
la descontaminación	decontamination
los residuos radioactivos	radioactive waste
los efectos nocivos	harmful effects
el reactor nuclear	nuclear reactor
la nocividad de las emisiones	the harmful nature of emissions
estar enterado/a de la amenaza	to be aware of the threat
los países nuclearizados	countries with nuclear capacity
reutilizar las bolsas de plástico	to reuse plastic bags
tirar las basuras al contenedor que les corresponde	to put rubbish into the correct bin
los envases de cartón	cardboard packaging
envenenar	to poison
venenoso/a	poisonous
la mancha de petróleo	oil slick
el reciclaje de los desperdicios/la basura	recycling of waste
reciclar	to recycle
La contaminación sonora	**Noise pollution**
el nivel sonoro máximo	maximum noise level
los trastornos auditivos	hearing disorders
la insonorización	soundproofing
insonorizar una casa	to soundproof a house

Websites

www.mapama.gob.es

www.greenpeace.org/espana (or other relevant country after the slash)

www.wwf.es

E.3 La moda — *Fashion*

Vocabulario clave	***Key vocabulary***
el/la modelo	(fashion) model
el/la diseñador(a)	designer
estar de moda	to be trendy/fashionable
el estilo	style
la marca	brand, label, make
la imagen (*pl* imágenes)	image, picture
llevar	to wear
vestirse	to get dressed
la tendencia	trend
el/la seguidor(a)	follower, fan
el/la aficionado/a	fan

En general	***In general***
la tendencia de la temporada	seasonal trend
las últimas tendencias de moda	latest fashion trends
las modas cambiantes	changing fashions
las novedades	latest products
la campaña publicitaria	advertising campaign
publicitario/a	advertising (*adj*)
la publicidad excesiva	advertising hype
el/la consumidor(a)	consumer
el consumo	consumption
el atractivo físico	physical attractiveness
la foto	photo
la portada de revista	magazine cover
promocionar	to publicise, to promote
la marca de moda	designer label
la última moda	the latest fashion
pasar de moda	to go out of fashion
pasado/a de moda	outdated, out of fashion
adicto/a a la moda	addicted to fashion
sentar bien	to suit
el diseño gráfico	graphic design
el/la diseñador(a) de moda	fashion designer
el/la sastre	tailor
el/la modista	dressmaker; fashion designer
el icono de moda	fashion icon

el/la asesor(a) de imagen	image consultant
el/la asesor(a) de estilo	lifestyle consultant
ejercer influencia en	to exert influence on

---

aparecer	to appear
destacar(se)	to stand out
formal	formal
informal	informal
la elegancia	elegance
elegante	elegant, fashionable
bello/a	beautiful
la belleza	beauty
bronceado/a	tanned
impactante	striking, impressive
glamuroso/a	glamorous
prestigioso/a	prestigious
vistoso/a	colourful, flashy
andrógino/a	androgenous
vanguardista	*avant-garde*
sobresaliente	outstanding
sobresalir	to stand/tower above
el peinado	hairstyle
el maquillaje	make-up
maquillarse	to (put on) make-up
el pintalabios	lipstick
el lápiz de ojos	eyebrow pencil
hacerse la cirurgía plástica/estética	to have plastic surgery

La expresión de uno mismo	***Expressing oneself***
Somos la ropa que usamos.	We are the clothes we wear.
expresar su personalidad en la ropa	to express one's personality in one's clothes
un estilo que refleja tus gustos/tu personalidad	a style that reflects your tastes/personality
ser fiel a cierta marca de ropa	to be loyal to a certain label
La compra de ropa de cierta marca provee un estatus.	Buying certain brands of clothes gives status.
seguir las tendencias del mercado	to follow market trends
identificarse con una marca	to identify with a brand
Las redes sociales son la plataforma esencial para las marcas.	Social networks are the key platform for brands.
estar conectado/a con el grupo	to be connected with the group

el código de vestimenta de su grupo	the dress-code of your group
conformarse	to conform
imitar lo que hacen los demás	to imitate what the others are doing
la sensación de pertenencia	feeling of belonging
sentirse excluido/a	to feel excluded
el rechazo	rejection
el rechazo del individuo por el grupo	rejection of the individual by the group
la falta de aceptación de los demás miembros del grupo	non-acceptance by the other members of the group

El modelaje	***Modelling***
el/la modelo de pasarela	catwalk model
el/la modelo de fotografía	photographic model
el/la modelo de talla grande	plus-size model
el/la supermodelo	supermodel
la talla	size
la estatura	height
la figura **el tipo** **la línea**	figure
las medidas	measurements
la cintura	waist
las caderas	hips
posar	to pose, to model
el porte	bearing, poise
la pasarela	catwalk
tener un buen aspecto	to look good
exhibir prendas de ropa	to display clothing
peinar a alguien	to style someone's hair
la sesión de fotos	photo shoot

Las presiones de la industria de la moda	***Pressures of the fashion industry***
el miedo a padecer sobrepeso	fear of being overwieght
la insatisfacción corporal	dissatisfaction with one's body
la obsesión por la silueta	obsessive concern with shape
las modelos flacas	skinny models
el ansia (*f*) de delgadez	yearning to be thin
la dieta **el régimen alimenticio**	diet
los trastornos de la alimentación	eating disorders
privarse de alimento	to go without food
la pérdida de peso	loss of weight

anoréxico/a	anorexic
la anorexia	anorexia
la bulimia	bulimia
adelgazar	to slim, to lose weight
engordar	to get fat, to put on weight
el temor a engordar	the fear of putting on weight
sentirse gordo/a	to feel fat
gordito/a	chubby, plump
la aerografía	airbrushing
usar el aerógrafo	to airbrush
La ropa	***Clothes***
el atuendo	attire, dress
lucir un nuevo vestido	to show off a new dress
estrenar un vestido	to wear a new dress
la ropa de diseño	designer clothes
la ropa lista para llevar	ready-to-wear clothes
la vestimenta	clothing
una prenda de vestir	a garment/an article of clothing

---

el sombrero	hat
la boina	beret
la gorra con visera	peaked cap
la capa la manta	cloak, gown
el chal	shawl, scarf
la bufanda	scarf
el velo	veil
la corbata	tie
el lazo	bow
el cuello	collar; neck
el abrigo de pieles	leather coat
la cazadora de cuero	leather jacket
la chaqueta la americana	jacket
la caída de la chaqueta	hang of a jacket
el jersey	jersey
el suéter	sweater
la camiseta	T-shirt
la blusa	blouse
la camisa a rayas	striped shirt

la manga	sleeve
el chaleco	waistcoat
el sujetador	bra
el camisón de noche	nightdress
la ropa interior	underclothes
el cinturón	belt
el pantalón vaquero **el pantalón tejano**	jeans
los vaqueros rotos	ripped jeans
la minifalda	miniskirt
las medias	tights
la sandalia	sandal
la alpargata	(rope) sandal
el calzado	footwear
la bota	boot
los zapatos	shoes
las zapatillas deportivas	sports shoes
las zapatillas	trainers
el tacón	heel
el tacón de aguja	stiletto heel
los tacones altos/bajos	high/low heels
el traje	suit
el corte de un traje	the cut of a suit
el traje de etiqueta	formal dress
el traje de baño **el bañador**	swimming costume

---

llevar puesto/a	to have on
ponerse (los zapatos, etc.)	to put on (shoes etc.)
vestirse de modo sugerente	to dress in a suggestive/sexy way
el escote	neckline, cleavage
la preocupación por vestir bien	the desire to be well-dressed
saber elegir lo más elegante	to know how to choose the smartest (clothes etc.)
vestirse de negro, etc.	to dress in black etc.
el vestuario exclusivo	exclusive wardrobe
probarse la ropa	to try on clothes
el botón	button
la cinta	ribbon
la cremallera	zip fastener
rayado/a	striped

holgado/a	loose, baggy
desenfadado/a	casual (in dress)
la alta costura	*haute couture*
Los accesorios	***Accessories***
los complementos de moda	fashion accessories
el anillo	ring
la bisutería	costume jewellery
el bolso	handbag
el bolso de cuero	leather handbag
el collar	necklace
las gafas de marca	designer glasses
las gafas de sol de moda	trendy sunglasses
los guantes	gloves
la joya	jewel
la marroquinería	leather goods
el pendiente	earring
la pulsera	bracelet, wristband
el reloj	watch
Las formas	***Shapes***
circular	circular
cuadrado/a	square
la línea	line
rectangular	rectangular
redondeado/a	round, rounded
triangular	triangular
Los tejidos	***Fabrics***
el algodón	cotton
el cuero	leather
la piel	leather, fur
la lana	wool
de lana	woollen
el lino	linen
el nilón	nylon
el satén	satin
la seda	silk
la tela	fabric, cloth
el terciopelo	velvet
el vaquero	denim

Sección F Algunos verbos útiles

The following is a selection of mainly abstract verbs that cannot be listed under particular theme headings but which are very useful in written and spoken argument.

to abolish	**eliminar, suprimir**
to get accustomed to	**acostumbrarse a**
to achieve	**conseguir**
to acknowledge (recognise)	**reconocer**
to act	**actuar (*in theatre*); actuar, obrar (*to do sth*)**
to add	**añadir**
to admit	**admitir (*all senses*); confesar (*confess*)**
to advise	**aconsejar**
to agree with	**ponerse/estar de acuerdo con**
to allow	**permitir**
to alter	**cambiar**
to annoy	**fastidiar, enojar**
to apologise	**disculparse**
to appreciate	**apreciar (*most senses*); valorar (*value*)**
to approve	**aprobar**
to assist	**ayudar**
to attempt	**intentar, probar**
to attract	**atraer**
to avenge (oneself)	**vengar(se)**
to avoid	**evitar**
to bear (endure)	**aguantar**
to behave	**comportarse**
to betray	**traicionar**
to blame	**culpar**
to borrow	**pedir prestado**
to cheat (deceive)	**burlar**
to check	**comprobar**
to choose	**escoger, elegir**
to command	**mandar, ordenar**
to compel	**obligar**
to complain	**quejarse, lamentarse**
to compose	**componer**
to conclude	**concluir**

to confuse	**confundir**
to congratulate (on)	**felicitar (por)**
to dare (to)	**atreverse a, osar**
to deal (with sth)	**tratar de**
to decrease, to diminish	**disminuir**
to demand	**exigir, reivindicar**
to deny	**negar**
to depend (on)	**depender (de)**
to deserve	**merecer**
to despise	**despreciar**
to develop	**desarrollar**
to disagree (object)	**no estar de acuerdo, oponerse**
to disappoint	**decepcionar**
to disgust	**dar asco**
to distrust	**desconfiar de, recelar**
to emphasise	**subrayar**
to envy	**envidiar**
to excuse	**perdonar**
to fail	**fracasar**
to favour	**favorecer**
to fear	**temer**
to fight (for)	**luchar (por)**
to forbid	**prohibir**
to forget	**olvidar**
to forgive	**perdonar**
to frighten	**asustar, dar un susto a**
to fulfil	**cumplir**
to govern	**gobernar**
to hate	**odiar, aborrecer**
to hesitate	**dudar, vacilar**
to hinder	**impedir, estorbar**
to imagine	**imaginarse, figurarse**
to improve	**mejorar**
to increase	**aumentar (*trans*), aumentarse (*intrans*)**
to influence	**influir en**
to intend to	**pensar**
to judge	**juzgar**
to loathe	**aborrecer**
to measure	**medir**
to make a mistake (be wrong)	**equivocarse**
to mistrust	**desconfiar de, recelar**

to mix	**mezclar**
to neglect	**descuidar, desatender**
to notice	**observar, notar**
to obey	**obedecer**
to object to	**oponerse a**
to offend	**ofender**
to offer	**ofrecer**
to owe	**deber**
to own	**poseer, ser dueño de**
to permit	**permitir**
to possess	**poseer**
to prejudice	**perjudicar**
to pretend (make believe)	**fingir**
to prevent	**impedir**
to profit from	**aprovechar de**
to promise	**prometer**
to propose	**proponer**
to protect	**proteger**
to prove	**comprobar**
to provide	**proveer, suministrar**
to quarrel	**reñir**
to recognise	**reconocer**
to refuse (to)	**negarse (a), rehusar**
to regret (be sorry for)	**sentir, lamentar**
to reject	**rechazar**
to rely on	**contar con, fiarse de**
to require	**exigir**
to resemble	**parecerse a**
to satisfy	**satisfacer**
to support	**apoyar**
to suppose	**suponer**
to suspect (of)	**sospechar (de)**
to thank	**agradecer**
to threaten (to/with)	**amenazar (con +** ***inf*** **or** ***n*****)**
to trust	**fiarse de**
to waste (money/resources)	**malgastar, despilfarrar**
to worry	**inquietarse, preocuparse**